Be My Disciples

Peter M. Esposito
President

Jo Rotunno, MA
Publisher

Susan Smith
Director of Project Development

Program Advisors
Michael P. Horan, PhD
Elizabeth Nagel, SSD

GRADE ONE
PARISH EDITION

The Subcommittee on the Catechism, United States Conference of Catholic Bishops, has found this catechetical series, copyright 2013, to be in conformity with the Catechism of the Catholic Church.

NIHIL OBSTAT
Rev. Msgr. Robert Coerver
Censor Librorum

IMPRIMATUR
† Most Reverend Kevin J. Farrell DD
Bishop of Dallas
August 22, 2011

The *Nihil Obstat and Imprimatur* are official declarations that the material reviewed is free of doctrinal or moral error. No implication is contained therein that those granting the *Nihil Obstat and Imprimatur* agree with the contents, opinions, or statements expressed.

Acknowledgements

Excerpts are taken and adapted from the *New American Bible* with Revised New Testament and Revised Psalms ©1991, 1986, 1970, Confraternity of Christian Doctrine, Washington, D.C., and are used by permission. All Rights Reserved. No part of the *New American Bible* may be reproduced in any form without permission in writing from the copyright owner.

Excerpts are taken or adapted from the English translation of the Rite of Baptism, ©1969; Rite of Confirmation (Second Edition), ©1975, International Committee on English in the Liturgy, Inc. (ICEL). All rights reserved.

Excerpts are taken and adapted from the English translation of the *Roman Missal*, ©2010, International Commission on English in the Liturgy, Inc. (ICEL) All rights reserved.

Toll Free   877-275-4725
Fax   800-688-8356

Visit us at www.RCLBenziger.com
and www.ByMyDisciples.com

20701 ISBN 978-0-7829-1570-9 (Student Edition)
20711 ISBN 978-0-7829-1576-1 (Catechist Edition)

1st printing
Manufactured for RCL Benziger in Cincinnati, OH, USA. December, 2011

Contents

Welcome to
Be My Disciples

Jesus wants you to be his **disciple**! He wants you to know about him and follow him. This year you will learn many new things about Jesus. You will learn how to be a good disciple.

All About Me
My name is

_____

- -

_____.

I am a child of God.

Unit 1: We Believe, Part One
You will learn about God's Son, Jesus.
Look on page 38. Find out the name of Jesus' mother.
Trace her name on the line.

_____

- - - Mary - - - - - - - - - - - - - - - - - - -

_____

Unit 2: We Believe, Part Two
You will learn about the Holy Trinity.
Look on page 66. Find out the name of the helper Jesus promised to send. Trace the helper's name on the line.

_____

- - Holy Spirit - - - - - - - - - - - - - - - - -

Unit 3: We Worship, Part One

You will learn that each of the Church's seasons tell us something about Jesus.

Look on page 87. Find out when the Church celebrates that Jesus was raised from the dead. Trace the word on the line.

Easter

Unit 4: We Worship, Part Two

You will learn how our Church celebrates and prays.

Look on page 137. Learn the name of the most important celebration of the Church. Trace the word on the line.

Mass

Unit 5: We Live, Part One

You will learn how to live the Ten Commandments.

Look on page 167. Learn which commandment teaches us to worship only God. Trace the word on the line.

First

Unit 6: We Live, Part Two

You will learn to live as a child of God.

Look on page 218. Learn who gave us the Our Father. Trace the name under the picture.

Jesus

Listen to God's Word

Leader
We gather to praise your Word,
O Lord.

All
**Happy are the people
who listen to God's Word.**
*(Listen while the Leader reads from
the Bible.)*

Leader
A reading from the Gospel
according to Luke.
(Proclaim Luke 19:1–10.)
The Gospel of the Lord.

All
Praise to you, Lord Jesus Christ.

Leader
Come forward in a line and bow
before the Bible.

Time for Children

The day was getting late. Jesus was tired. His friends wanted him to rest. But moms and dads started bringing their children to see Jesus. Jesus' friends said to them, "Go away. Jesus is tired. He has no time for children now."

"Wait!" Jesus said to his friends. "I always have time for children. Let the children come to me."

The children rushed to Jesus. Jesus welcomed and blessed them all. Jesus said with a big smile, "Look, this is what heaven is like."

BASED ON MARK 10:13–16

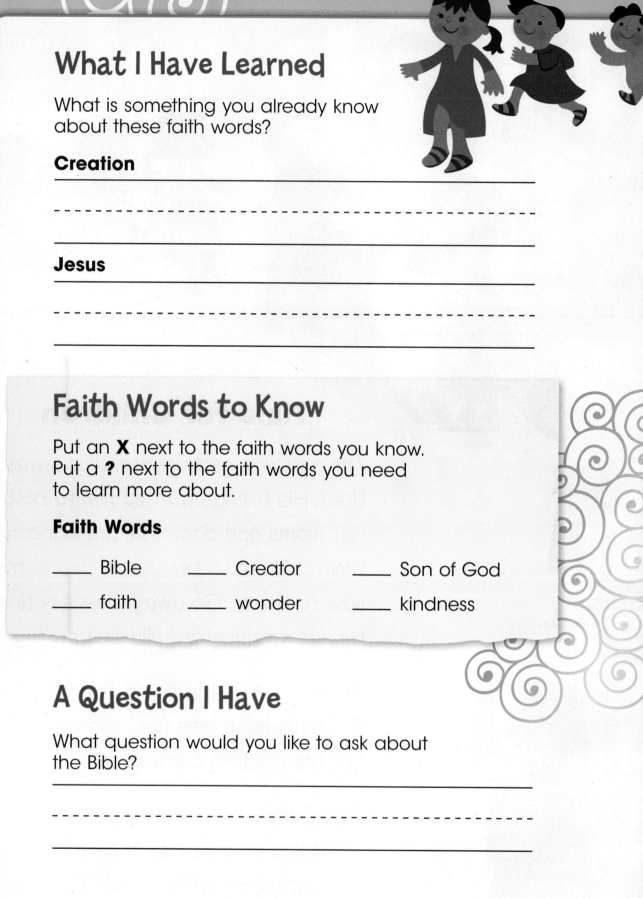

What I Have Learned

What is something you already know about these faith words?

Creation

_____

- -

_____

Jesus

_____

- -

_____

Faith Words to Know

Put an **X** next to the faith words you know.
Put a **?** next to the faith words you need
to learn more about.

Faith Words

____ Bible   ____ Creator   ____ Son of God

____ faith   ____ wonder   ____ kindness

A Question I Have

What question would you like to ask about
the Bible?

_____

- -

_____

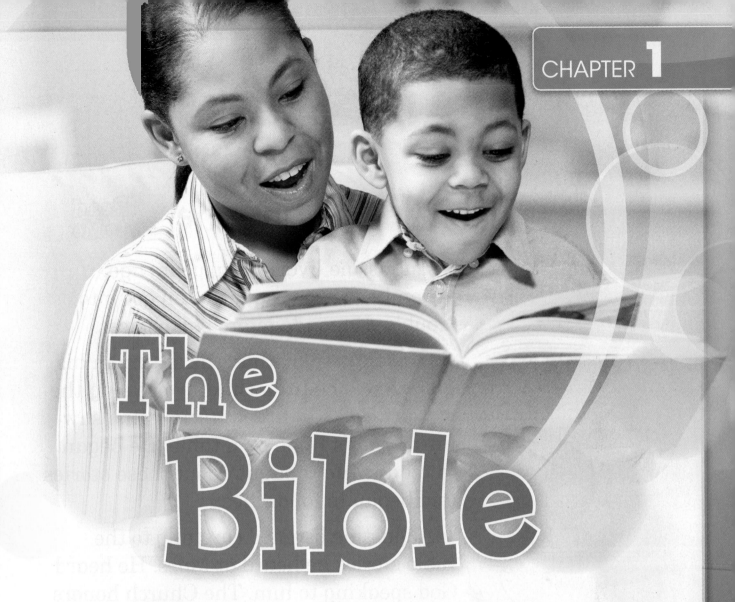

CHAPTER 1

The Bible

? **What is a favorite book that someone reads to you?**
Why is it your favorite?

When we listen to a story from the Bible, we hear God's Word to us. In the Bible we read:

Listen to God's word and keep it.

Then you will be blessed.   BASED ON LUKE 11:28

? **What do these words from the Bible ask you to do?**

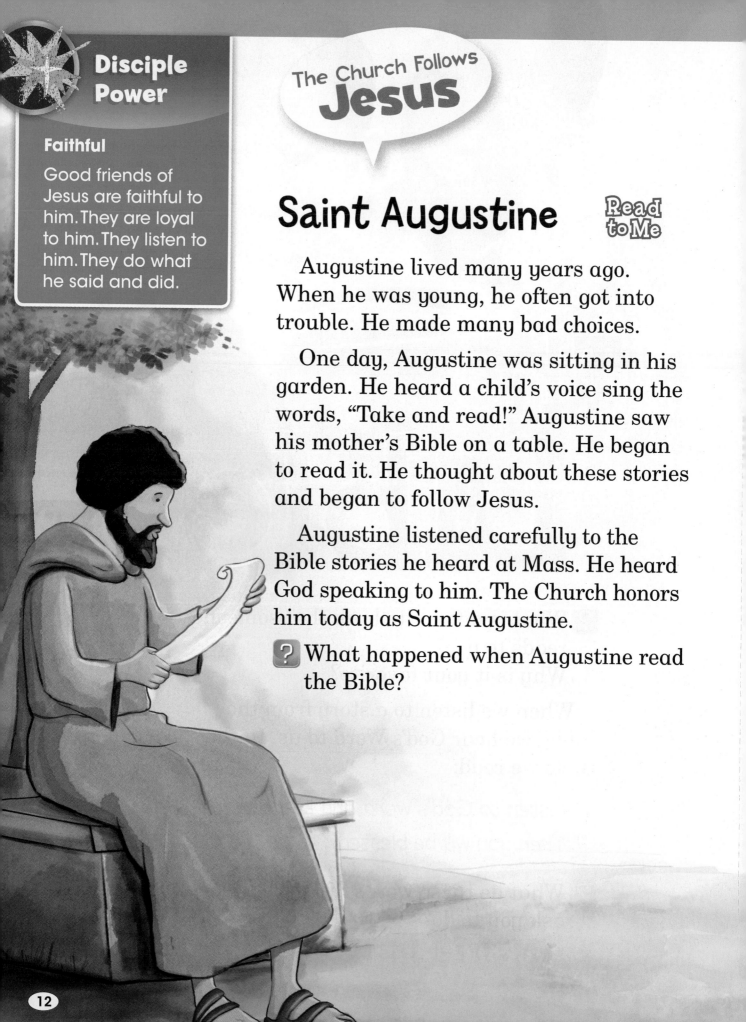

Faithful

Good friends of Jesus are faithful to him. They are loyal to him. They listen to him. They do what he said and did.

The Church Follows **Jesus**

Saint Augustine

Read to Me

Augustine lived many years ago. When he was young, he often got into trouble. He made many bad choices.

One day, Augustine was sitting in his garden. He heard a child's voice sing the words, "Take and read!" Augustine saw his mother's Bible on a table. He began to read it. He thought about these stories and began to follow Jesus.

Augustine listened carefully to the Bible stories he heard at Mass. He heard God speaking to him. The Church honors him today as Saint Augustine.

? What happened when Augustine read the Bible?

About the Bible

God chose people to help write the **Bible**. The Bible is the written Word of God. It is a holy book because it is God's very own Word to us. The Bible also tells us about God's love for us.

Faith Focus
What does the Bible tell us about God?

Faith Word
Bible
The Bible is the written Word of God. It is God's very own Word to us.

Activity Draw or write about your favorite story from the Bible. Share your story with a partner.

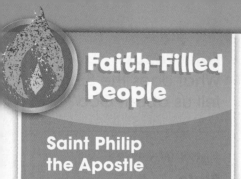

Faith-Filled People

Saint Philip the Apostle

Philip was one of the first twelve Apostles. The Apostles were the first leaders of the Church. Philip was a curious man. He wanted to know everything he could about Jesus and his teachings.

A Man Learns about God

One day a man was reading the Bible. Philip was a follower, or disciple, of Jesus. He saw the man and ran up to him.

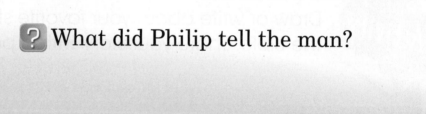

Philip asked, "Do you understand what you are reading?"

The man said. "No. I need help."

Philip told the man about God's love.

Philip told the man about Jesus.

The man became a follower of Jesus.

He became a member of the Church.

BASED ON ACTS OF THE APOSTLES 8:26–40

❓ What did Philip tell the man?

Learning about God

Philip helped the man to understand a story in the Bible. He helped the man become a follower of Jesus.

At Mass, we listen to readings from the Bible. The priest or deacon helps us understand what we heard. This helps us learn how to follow Jesus.

Activity

When the Bible is read to you, what do you do? Trace the dotted lines to find out.

listen

I Follow Jesus

The Bible is God's Word to you. When you listen to the Bible at Mass, God is speaking to you. When you and your family read the Bible at home, God is speaking to you. When you do these things, you are a faithful and loyal follower of Jesus.

Activity

Reading God's Word

Draw you and your family reading the Bible at home.

My Faith Choice

Check (√) how you will listen to God speaking to you in the Bible.

This week I will

☐ listen to the readings at Mass.

☐ ask someone to read a Bible story to me.

 Pray, "Thank you, Holy Spirit, for helping me listen to the Word of God and follow Jesus. Amen."

Chapter Review

Draw lines to finish the sentences.

1. The Bible tells us about   Word of God.

2. We hear the Word of God   God's love for us.

3. The Bible is the written   follow Jesus.

4. Augustine read the Bible and began to   at Mass.

▶ TO HELP YOU REMEMBER

1. The Bible is God's Word to us.

2. Stories in the Bible teach us about God's love.

3. We listen to the Bible at Mass.

A Listening Prayer

Leader   O God, open our ears.
Help us listen to your Word.

All   **Help us listen to your Word.**

Leader   Listen to the Word of God.
Then think about what you hear.

Reader   Act as children of God.
Obey your parents. Love others,
just as Jesus did.

         BASED ON EPHESIANS 5:1, 6:1

Reader   *Hold up the Bible and say:*
The Word of the Lord.

All   **Thanks be to God.**

With My Family

This Week . . .

In chapter 1, "The Bible," your child learned:

▶ God is the real author of the Bible.

▶ The Bible is the inspired, written Word of God.

▶ The Holy Spirit inspired the human writers of the Bible to assure that God's Word would be accurately communicated.

▶ A faithful follower of Jesus reads the Bible and follows the teachings of the Church.

For more about related teachings of the Church, see the *Catechism of the Catholic Church*, 101–133, and the *United States Catholic Catechism for Adults*, pages 11–15.

■ Sharing God's Word

Read together Acts of the Apostles 8:26–40 about Philip the Apostle. Or read the adaptation of the story on page 14. Talk about why it is important to read the Bible every day.

■ We Live as Disciples

The Christian home and family is a school of discipleship. Choose one or more of the following activities to do as a family or design a similar activity of your own.

▶ Throughout the week choose a time to read the Bible as a family. Talk about ways the Bible passage or story you read helps your family live as a Catholic family.

▶ Help your child develop good habits that help him or her become a faithful follower of Jesus. Build on the things your child is already doing; for example, praying each day, helping out at home with chores, or treating others kindly.

■ Our Spiritual Journey

In this section, you will learn some of the major spiritual disciplines of the Church. These disciplines help us form the good habits of living as faithful followers of Jesus. Daily prayer is one of those disciplines. In this chapter, your child prayed and listened to Scripture. Read and pray together the prayer on page 17. This type of prayer is called *lectio divina*.

For more ideas on ways your family can live as disciples of Jesus, visit **www.BeMyDisciples.com**

CHAPTER 2

God Loves Us

? Name the people who know and love you. How do they show you that they love you?

The Bible tells us that God loves us. Listen to these words from the Bible about God's love for you.

Lord, you see me and know me.

You know when I sit and when I stand.

You know what I think and where I go.

You know everything I do.   BASED ON PSALM 139:1–6

? What do these words say about God?

The Church Follows **Jesus**

Generosity

Followers of Jesus are generous. We share our things with others. We pray for them. We show generosity to them.

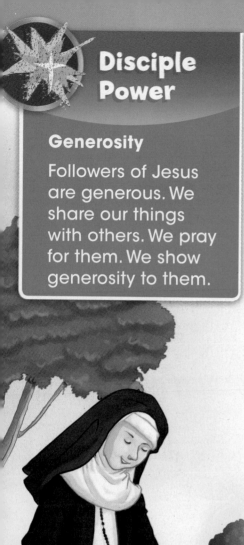

Saint Rose of Lima

Read to Me

Rose knew and loved God. She knew that God loved her. She helped others know about God's love.

Rose lived with her family in Lima in the country of Peru. Rose helped take care of the family garden. She grew flowers and food. She sold flowers and gave the money to the poor and the sick. This made them feel better.

Rose was kind and generous. She helped people learn how much God loved them.

Saint Rose of Lima shows us how to love God and help others. You can pray to Saint Rose. Ask her to help you share God's love too.

Activity

Dear Saint Rose,

Help me to show my love for

_____

- -

_____

We Know God Loves Us

Faith Focus
Who helps us to know God and believe in him?

God knows us and loves us all the time.

God wants us to know and love him too.

The Bible has many stories of people who had **faith** in God. They listened to God. They came to know and **believe** in him.

Here is a Bible story about faith. Abraham and Sarah lived a long time before Jesus. God chose Abraham to be a great leader. God made him a promise. God said,

Faith Words

faith
Faith is a gift from God. It helps us to know God and to believe in him.

believe
To believe means to have faith in God. It means to give yourself to God with all your heart.

> You will be the father of many nations. I will bless you and your wife Sarah. You will soon become the parents of a son.
>
> BASED ON GENESIS 17:4, 15–16

Abraham and Sarah listened to God and did what he asked. They had faith in God and believed in his promises.

❓ What did God promise Abraham?

Faith-Filled People

Isaac

Isaac is the son whom God promised Abraham and Sarah. The name Isaac means "he laughs." Isaac brought much joy and happiness to his parents.

Jesus Helps Us to Know God

Many years after Abraham and Sarah died, God sent his Son Jesus to us. Jesus is the Son of God.

Jesus helps us best to know God and his love. Jesus helps us to believe in God and have faith in him.

Jesus taught over and over again how much God loves us. He taught us that God is love.

Activity Color the spaces. Make the **X**s one color and the **O**s another color. Find out who teaches us the most about God.

22

Our Family Helps Us Know God

God gave us the gift of a family. Our families help us grow in our faith. They help us know God and believe in him. Our families help us give ourselves to God with all our hearts.

Activity

Trace the words. Discover one important thing about God.

God
loves us.

23

I Follow Jesus

Your family and the Church help you to learn how much God loves you. You can help your family and friends learn how much God loves them. You can treat them the way Jesus asked. You can be kind and generous to them.

Activity

Sharing God's Love

In one heart, draw people helping you learn about God. In the second heart, draw yourself sharing God's love.

My Faith Choice

Check (√) what will you do. This week I will help others know how much God loves them. I will

- ☐ tell others about God.
- ☐ show my family I love them.
- ☐ thank God for his love.

Pray, "Thank you, Holy Spirit, for helping me to show my love for God. Amen."

Chapter Review

Complete the sentences. Color the ☐ next to the best choice.

1. To _____ means to have faith in God.

 believe

☐ hope

2. Faith is a gift from _____.

☐ our friends

☐ God

▶ **TO HELP YOU REMEMBER**

1. God's gift of faith helps us come to know him and believe in him.

2. Jesus is the Son of God. He helps us to know how much God loves us and to have faith in God.

3. Our family and our Church help us to know, love, and serve God.

Sign of the Cross

We pray the Sign of the Cross to begin our prayers. Pray the Sign of the Cross with your class.

 In the name of the Father,

 and of the Son,

 and of the Holy Spirit.

 Amen.

With My Family

This Week . . .

In chapter 2, "God Loves Us," your child learned:

▶ God has revealed himself and invites us to believe in him and his love for us.

▶ Jesus Christ reveals the most about God and his love for us.

▶ Jesus is the Son of God. He is the fullness of God's Revelation.

▶ Our family and our Church help us grow in faith in God and in love for him.

For more about related teachings of the Church, see the *Catechism of the Catholic Church*, 80–95 and 142–175, and the *United States Catholic Catechism for Adults*, pages 35–47.

◼ Sharing God's Word

Read together John 13:31-35 from your family Bible or from a children's version of the Bible. Emphasize that when we treat one another as Jesus told his disciples to do, we show our love for God and for one another. We also show others how much God loves them.

◼ We Live as Disciples

The Christian home and family is a school of discipleship. It is the first place where children learn to live as disciples. Choose one or more of the following activities to do as a family or design a similar activity of your own.

▶ Compile a list of the names of people who have helped or who are helping your family grow in faith and in your love for God. Pray for these people at a family meal.

▶ Name the ways your family is generous to each other and to other people. Remind your children that when they are generous they are living as Jesus taught.

◼ Our Spiritual Journey

Generosity is a habit of being a disciple of Jesus. Generously sharing our spiritual and material blessings with others, especially people in need, is one of the foundational spiritual disciplines, or practices, of the Christian life. This discipline is known as almsgiving. Make almsgiving one of the hallmarks of your family's life. Pray together: Dear Jesus, give me a generous heart.

For more ideas on ways your family can live as disciples of Jesus, visit **www.BeMyDisciples.com**

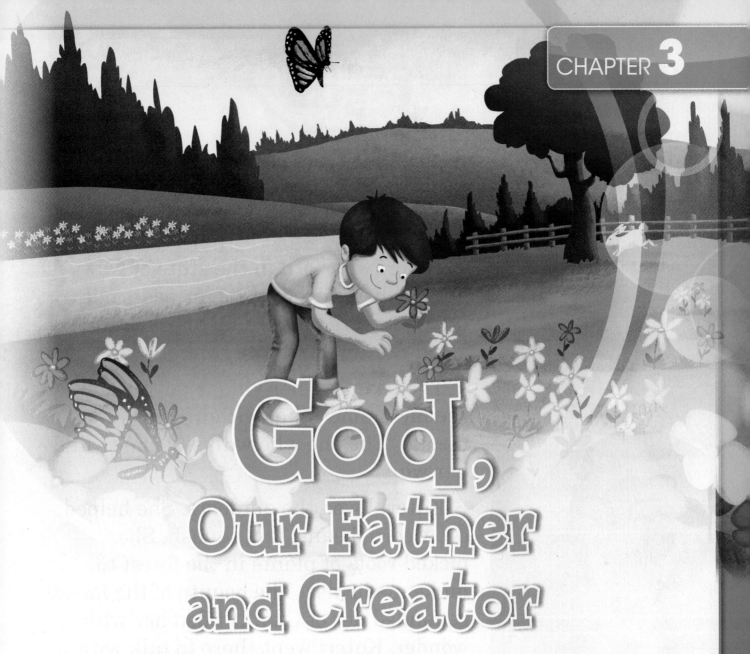

CHAPTER 3

God, Our Father and Creator

? What is your favorite part of creation?

Close your eyes and see all the beautiful things in the world. Listen to what the Bible tells us about the world.

O God, everything you made is wonderful!

BASED ON PSALM 136:4

? What do these words from the Bible tell you about the world God made?

Wonder

The word "wonderful" comes from the word "wonder." Wonder is a special gift from God. God gives us this gift to help us come to know how good he is.

The Church Follows **Jesus**

Kateri Tekakwitha

Kateri was born in the state of New York. When Kateri was four years old, her eyes were harmed by an illness. She could hardly see in the sunlight.

The people of her village gave Kateri the nickname Tekakwitha. This name means "The one who walks trying to find her way."

Kateri loved the outdoors. She helped grow corn, beans, and squash. She picked roots of plants in the forest to make medicines. The beauty of the forest reminded her of God. It filled her with wonder. Kateri went there to talk with God and listen to him.

The Catholic Church honors her as Blessed Kateri Tekakwitha. The things she did and said show us how to live as disciples of Jesus.

? Why was being in the forest important to Kateri?

God Made Everything

God is the **Creator** of the world.
God alone made Heaven and Earth.
He made everything out of love.
The Bible tells us,

God looked at everything he made.
He saw that it was very good.

BASED ON GENESIS 1:31

Activity Think of your favorite part of God's creation. Draw a picture of it. Share what it tells you about God.

Catherine of Siena

Catherine enjoyed looking at creation. Things in nature reminded Catherine how much God loves us. This helped her to grow in her love for God. The Church celebrates the feast day of Saint Catherine of Siena on April 29.

God Creates People

God is the Creator of all people. He creates every person to be an **image of God.** In the Bible we read,

God made people in his image. He blessed them and told them to take care of everything he made. God said everything he made was very good.

BASED ON GENESIS 1:26–31

God loves every person. We are very special to God. He created us to be happy with him now on Earth and forever in Heaven.

? Why are you special to God?

God Is Our Loving Father

Every person is created by God. God the Creator is our loving Father.

This is why the Bible tells us we are children of God.

Jesus helped us to know and believe that God is our Father. He taught us to pray, "Our Father, who art in heaven . . ."

BASED ON LUKE 11:2

God the Father loves us and knows each of us by name. Jesus told us that God the Father cares for all his creation. He cares for all people.

We show we love God our Father when we take care of ourselves. We show our love for God when we take care of creation.

Activity

Check (√) the ways you show your love for God.

God Loves Me. I Love God.

- ☐ I clean up trash.
- ☐ I get enough sleep.
- ☐ I am kind to pets.
- ☐ I do my best in school.

I Follow Jesus

God is wonderful. He is so very good to us. The world shows us how wonderful God is. The world is God's gift to everybody. One way you can say thank you to God is to help take care of the things in the world.

Activity

Caring for God's Creation

In the puzzle piece, draw a picture of yourself taking care of something in God's creation.

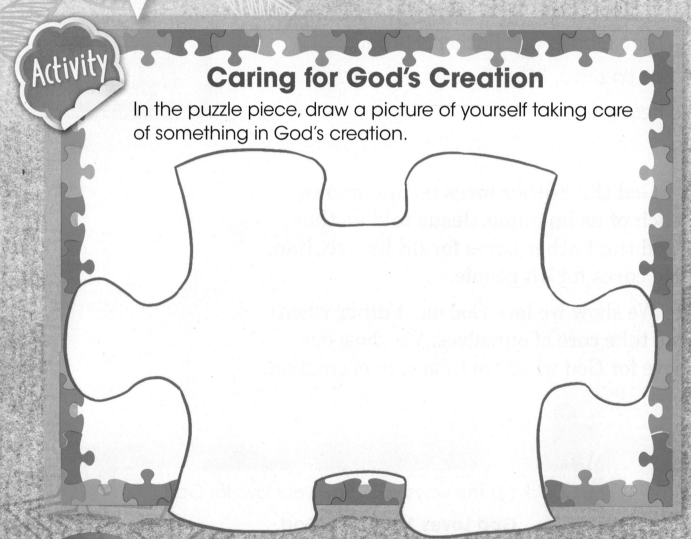

My Faith Choice

This week I will take care of God's creation. I will try to do what I have drawn in the puzzle.

 Pray, "Thank you, God. Thank you for the gift of your creation. Amen."

Chapter Review

Draw lines to complete the sentences.

Column A

1. Jesus
2. People
3. God

Column B

made everything out of love.

taught us to call God our Father.

are made in the image of God.

Thank You, God!

A rebus prayer uses pictures to help us pray.
Use a word for each picture. Pray the prayer together.

ALL **Thank you, God, for your .**

Reader 1 You made the and .

ALL **Thank you, God, for your .**

Reader 2 You made and  .

ALL **Thank you, God, for your .**

Reader 3 You made the  .

ALL **Thank you, God, for your .**
You made ME! Based on Psalm 148

With My Family

This Week . . .

In chapter 3, "God, Our Father and Creator," your child learned:

▶ God is the Creator. All God's creation is good. Everything good exists because God created it out of love.

▶ God created every person in his image. He created people with all their differences.

▶ God is our Father. There is no limit to his love for his children.

▶ We respond to God the Creator's love by helping to take care of creation.

For more about related teachings of the Church, see the *Catechism of the Catholic Church*, 232–248 and 268–314, and the *United States Catholic Catechism for Adults*, pages 53–56, 67–68.

■ Sharing God's Word

Read together the Bible story in Genesis 1:26–31 about the creation of people. Or read the adaptation of the story on page 30. Emphasize that every person is an image of God.

■ We Live as Disciples

The Christian home and family is a school of discipleship. It is the first place where children learn to live as disciples. Choose one or more of the following activities to do as a family or design a similar activity of your own.

▶ God created each person out of love. Take turns sharing what you like about each person.

▶ Invite your child to take part in keeping your home clean. Explain how this is one way of thanking God for his many gifts to your family.

■ Our Spiritual Journey

Prayer is one of the main spiritual disciplines of the Christian life. Giving thanks to God is one of the five main forms of prayer. Invite everyone to close their eyes and see their favorite part of creation. Think of how much God loves us and silently pray, "God you are so wonderful."

For more ideas on ways your family can live as disciples of Jesus, visit **www.BeMyDisciples.com**

CHAPTER 4

Jesus, the Son of God

[?] How do you celebrate your birthday?

Birthdays are wonderful days. Saint Luke tells us about the birthday of Jesus. He tells us:

Mary and Joseph came to Bethlehem. They had to stay in a stable with animals. During the night, Jesus was born. Mary wrapped him in cloth. She laid him in a manger. BASED ON LUKE 2:1–7

[?] What else do you know about the birth of Jesus?

Kindness

We live the virtue of kindness by treating others as we want to be treated.

The Church Follows **Jesus**

We Have Room!

Read to Me

Daniella and everyone in San Carlos was excited. It was almost time for Christmas. It was time to celebrate Las Posadas.

For nine nights, the people walked together in the streets. Two people were chosen to be Mary and Joseph. Everyone walked behind them. They carried lighted candles.

Mary and Joseph knocked on many doors. Joseph said, "My wife will soon have a baby. Do you have room for us in your home?" All answered, "We have no room." Finally, one family said to Joseph, "We have room! Come in."

Daniella was very excited. Her family was the one who answered, "We have room! Come in."

? How did Daniella and her family show kindness to Mary and Joseph?

The Son of God

At Christmas each year we remember and celebrate the birth of Jesus. Jesus is the only son of Mary and the **Son of God**. Jesus is truly God and truly man.

The Bible tells us that angels told shepherds about the birth of Jesus. We read,

The shepherds rushed and found Mary, Joseph, and Jesus. They told everyone about Jesus and praised God for all they heard and saw.

BASED ON LUKE 2:15–17, 20

Faith Focus
Who is Jesus?

Faith Words
Son of God
Jesus is the Son of God. Jesus is truly God and truly man.

Holy Family
The Holy Family is the family of Jesus, Mary, and Joseph.

Activity

Draw a picture of you telling others about Jesus. Do what the shepherds did.

The Holy Family

Mary is the mother of Jesus, the Son of God. Joseph is the foster father of Jesus. We call Jesus, Mary, and Joseph the **Holy Family**. The Holy Family lived in a town called Nazareth.

Mary and Joseph showed their love for Jesus. They took very good care of Jesus as he was growing up. Jesus grew in his love of God and of people.

Activity

Write the names *Jesus, Mary,* and *Joseph* under their pictures.

Jesus Shares God's Love

When Jesus grew up, he taught others about God. He shared God's love with everyone. Jesus showed us how to treat people. Jesus treated everyone with kindness and respect.

Respect means to treat every person as a child of God. We are to treat everyone with kindness and respect. We are to share God's love with people.

Activity

Color the ♡s in the photos of people showing kindness and respect.

I Follow Jesus

God is always kind to people. Jesus shared God's kindness with people. You are a disciple of Jesus. You are kind to people. You treat them with respect. When you do these things, you are a sign of God's love.

Activity In the kite draw yourself being kind to someone.

I Am Kind

My Faith Choice

This week I will do what I drew in the kite. I will

_____

- -

_____

Pray, "Thank you, Holy Spirit, for helping me to be kind to others as Jesus taught. Amen."

Chapter Review

Circle the word that best completes each sentence.

1. Jesus is the _____ of God.

    (Son)   Angel

2. _____ is the mother of Jesus.

    Anne   Mary

3. _____ is the foster father of Jesus.

    Joachim   Joseph

▶ **TO HELP YOU REMEMBER**

1. Jesus is the only son of Mary and the Son of God.

2. The family of Jesus, Mary, and Joseph is the Holy Family.

3. Jesus shared God's love with everyone.

Jesus, I Love You

We show that we love Jesus by treating people as he did. Learn to sign this prayer.

"Jesus, I love you."

Pray this prayer in the morning and at night. Teach your family to sign the prayer. Ask them to pray it with you.

Jesus

I love you.

With My Family

This Week . . .

In chapter 4, "Jesus, the Son of God," your child learned:

▶ Jesus is the only son of Mary and the Son of God.

▶ Gabriel announced to Mary that she would become the mother of the Savior, the Son of God who she was to name Jesus.

▶ The Son of God became truly human without giving up being God. This mystery of faith is called the Incarnation. Jesus is truly God and truly man.

▶ We call Jesus, Mary, and Joseph the Holy Family. Jesus' life in the Holy Family prepared him for the work the Father sent him to do.

For more about related teachings of the Church, see the *Catechism of the Catholic Church*, 456–478 and 512–560, and the *United States Catholic Catechism for Adults*, pages 77–87, 143–149.

▆ Sharing God's Word

Read together Luke 2:1–20 about the shepherds who rushed to see the newly born Jesus. Or read the adaptation of the story on page 37. Emphasize that Jesus is truly God and truly man. He is the only son of Mary and the Son of God.

▆ We Live as Disciples

The Christian home and family is a school of discipleship. Choose one or more of the following activities to do as a family or design a similar activity of your own.

▶ Talk together about the ways that family members are kind to each other. Explain how acts and words of kindness show a person's love for God.

▶ Choose to do a family activity that shows kindness to people who are not members of your family. For example, as a family visit someone who is lonely or help an elderly neighbor.

▆ Our Spiritual Journey

The Great Commandment is the guiding precept of the Christian life. It is the summary or foundational principle of human as well as Christian living. In this chapter your child signed an act of love using American Sign Language. Encourage your child to teach you to sign the prayer on page 41. Pray it often together.

For more ideas on ways your family can live as disciples of Jesus, visit **www.BeMyDisciples.com**

Unit 1 Review

A. Choose the Best Word

Complete the sentences. Color the circle next to the best choice.

1. The Bible is _____ own Word to us.

⭕ the Church's ⭕ God's

2. Faith is a gift from God that helps us to know

God and to _____ in him.

⭕ love ⭕ believe

3. Jesus treated _____ people with respect.

⭕ all ⭕ some

4. Jesus is the _____ of God.

⭕ Man ⭕ Son

5. _____ is the Mother of Jesus.

⭕ Mary ⭕ Anne

B. Show What You Know

Circle the numbers next to the words that tell about Jesus.

1. Son of God

2. Holy Spirit

3. Loving Father

4. taught others about God

5. shared God's love with everyone

C. Connect with Scripture

What was your favorite story about Jesus in this unit? Draw something that happened in the story. Tell your class about it.

D. Be a Disciple

1. *What saint or holy person did you enjoy hearing about in this unit? Write the name here. Tell your class what this person did to follow Jesus.*

_____

- -

_____

_____

- -

_____

2. *What can you do to be a good disciple of Jesus?*

_____

- -

_____

_____

- -

_____

The Last Supper

On the night before he died, Jesus ate a special meal with his Apostles. Here is what Jesus said and did.

Jesus took some bread. He gave thanks to God. He broke the bread. He shared the bread with his friends and said, "Eat this bread. It is my body."

Then Jesus took a cup filled with wine. He gave the cup to his friends and said, "Take this and drink. This is the cup of my blood. When you eat this bread and drink this wine, you remember me."

BASED ON 1 CORINTHIANS 11:23–26

What I Have Learned

What is something you already know about these faith words?

Mary

_____

- -

_____

The Holy Trinity

_____

- -

_____

Faith Words to Know

Put an **X** next to the faith words you know.
Put a **?** next to the faith words you need
to learn more about.

Faith Words

_____ angels   _____ hope   _____ Church

_____ courage   _____ Holy Spirit   _____ Catholic

A Question I Have

What question would you like to ask about
the Church?

_____

- -

_____

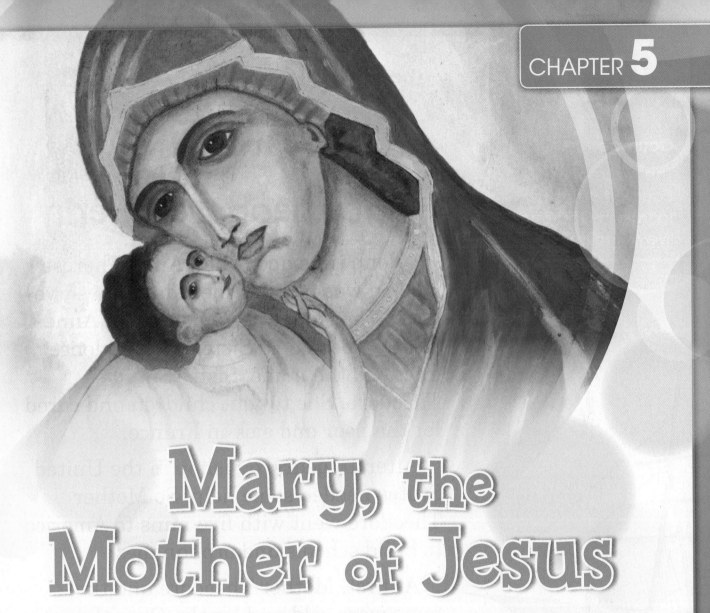

CHAPTER 5

Mary, the Mother of Jesus

? What is your favorite family story?

In the Bible, we hear stories about Mary. The angel Gabriel said to Mary:

Hail Mary, God is with you.

BASED ON LUKE 1:42

? What do these words from the Bible tell you about God?

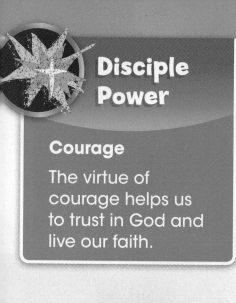

Disciple Power

Courage

The virtue of courage helps us to trust in God and live our faith.

The Church Follows **Jesus**

Read to Me

Saint Théodore Guérin

A long time ago, when Anne-Thérèse Guérin was a child, she wanted to serve God. When she was 25 years-old, Anne-Thérèse became a Sister of Providence and took the name, Sister Saint Théodore. She taught children and cared for the poor and sick in France.

After 16 years, a bishop in the United States needed some help. So Mother Théodore went with five nuns to America to build schools and orphanages.

At first, Mother Théodore and the nuns were cold and lonely. Over the years, people learned to trust the sisters. Like Mary, Mother Théodore lived a life of courage. She always trusted God.

The Church honors Mother Théodore Guérin as a saint and celebrates her feast day on October 3.

? How do you show that you trust God?

God Loves Mary

Angels are messengers of God. God sent the angel Gabriel to a young woman named Mary. The angel gave Mary this message from God. Gabriel said,

"You are blessed, Mary. The Holy Spirit will come to you. You will have a baby. The baby's name will be Jesus. He will be called the Son of God."

Mary listened carefully to the angel Gabriel. Then she said to Gabriel, "Yes, I will do what God wants me to do."

BASED ON LUKE 1:28, 31, 35, 38

Faith Focus
What does the Bible tell us about Mary?

Faith Word
angels
Angels give honor and glory to God. They are God's messengers and helpers.

Activity

Find a partner. Act out what happened when the angel Gabriel gave Mary the message from God. One of you will take the part the angel. One of you will be Mary.

Juan Diego walked many miles to Mass everyday. One day, Mary appeared to him on Tepeyac Hill. She told Juan to build a church on this site and sent him to the bishop. Soon a church was built. People from all over the world visit Mary's church.

Say Yes to God

Mary said yes to God. Mary had faith in God and trusted him. Mary loved God with her whole heart.

God asks us to have faith in him too. God asks us to trust him and to love him with our whole heart.

We have faith and trust that God will always be with us. We trust that God always loves us. We show we love God when we say yes to him as Mary did.

Activity

Check (√) ways you can say yes to God. I say yes to God when I

___ Pray every day.　　___ Share my toys.

___ Act mean.　　___ Play fairly.

___ Help at home.　　___ Say "Thank you."

God Chose Mary

God chose Mary to be the mother of Jesus. Mary cared for Jesus. We call Mary the Mother of God. Mary is very special.

Jesus wants Mary to love and care for us, too. He gave her to us as our special mother. Mary prays for us.

We celebrate the feast of Mary, the Mother of God on January 1. She prays to her son, Jesus, for us.

? Why is Mary our special mother?

Catholics Believe

Feast Days

The Church honors and shows our love for Mary on special days each year. These are called feast days. Each year on January 1 we celebrate the feast of Mary, the Mother of God. This is a holy day of obligation. We have the responsibility to take part in the celebration of Mass.

I Follow Jesus

Mary showed her faith and love for God. Courage can help you show your faith in God. You show your faith and love for God by what you say and what you do.

Activity

I Trust in God

Choose one way you can show your courage as a follower of Jesus. Draw or write about it in this space.

My Faith Choice

This week I will show my faith and love for God. I will

_____

- -

_____

Pray, "Thank you, God, for helping me to show my faith and love for you."

Chapter Review

Complete the sentences. Color the ◯ next to the best choice .

1. Mary said, "___" to God.

   ◉ Yes   ◯ No

2. Courage helps us to ___ God.

   ◯ trust   ◯ know

3. Saint Juan Diego walked to ___ every day.

   ◯ school   ◯ Mass

Psalm Prayer

Psalms are prayers in the Bible. We pray a psalm during Mass. Pray together:

Leader   We listen to God's Word, like Mary.

Happy are the people who listen to God's Word.   BASED ON PSALM 1:1–2

All   **Happy are the people who listen to God's Word.**

Leader   We say yes to God, like Mary.

All   **Happy are the people who listen to God's Word.**

With My Family

This Week . . .

In chapter 5, "Mary, the Mother of Jesus," your child learned:

▶ The Gospel account of the Annunciation tells us about the angel Gabriel announcing to Mary that God had chosen her to be the mother of Jesus.

▶ Mary is the mother of Jesus, the Son of God. Mary is the Mother of God.

▶ The Gospel account of the Annunciation shares with us Mary's faith and trust in God and her love for him.

▶ Courage helps us trust in God and live our faith, even in difficult times.

For more about related teachings of the Church, see the *Catechism of the Catholic Church*, 484–507, and the *United States Catholic Catechism for Adults*, pages 141–149.

◼ Sharing God's Word

Read together Luke 1:26–38, the Gospel account of the Annunciation. Or read the adaptation of the story on page 48. Emphasize Mary's faith and trust in God and her love for him.

◼ We Live as Disciples

The Christian home and family is a school of discipleship. Choose one or more of the following activities to do as a family or design a similar activity of your own.

▶ Teach your child the Mass responses "Thanks be to God" and "Praise to you, Lord Jesus Christ." Guide your child to use these responses properly when your family takes part in the celebration of the Mass.

▶ Courage is the virtue that helps us trust God and live our faith. Help your child to recognize the ways your family is living this virtue. Remind them that when they say yes to God, they are living as disciples of Jesus.

◼ Our Spiritual Journey

The Psalms are a confession of faith in song. From the times of David until the present, the praying of the Psalms has nourished the faith of the People of God. Such prayer is both personal and communal. Memorize psalm verses such as the one on page 53 and integrate praying them spontaneously to respond to the various circumstances of your life.

For more ideas on ways your family can live as disciples of Jesus, visit **www.BeMyDisciples.com**

CHAPTER 6

Jesus Shares God's Love

? How do family members show love for one another?

Jesus always shares God's love with people. He said,

"Let the children come to me. If you want to enter God's Kingdom, become like a child." Then Jesus took the children in his arms and blessed them.

BASED ON MARK 10:14–16

? How do you show others that God loves them?

Hope

The virtue of hope helps us to remember that one day we may live in happiness with God forever in Heaven.

The Church Follows **Jesus**

Saint Gianna

Read to Me

Saint Gianna Beretta Molla was a wife, a mother, and a doctor. She cared for many people in her life. They all remembered her smile and her care for others.

Gianna believed that caring for the sick showed God's love. If her patients did not have money to pay her, she let them give her food. Sometimes she paid for their medicine herself.

Gianna was a doctor who cared for children. She helped mothers learn how to take care of themselves and their children.

In 1955 Gianna married Pietro Molla and soon they had three children. She helped them and all people have hope in God.

? Who are some of the people who share God's love with you?

Jesus Loves Us

Jesus always shared God's love with people. He helped people in many ways. Jesus forgave the people who hurt him.

Some people did not want Jesus to teach and help others. They had Jesus killed on a **cross**. This is called the Crucifixion.

Because he loved us, Jesus died on a cross for all of us. He forgave the people who put him on the cross. He forgives us when we sin. Jesus died so that we could live with him forever in Heaven.

Activity

Trace the words. Pray the prayer with a partner to thank Jesus for his love.

Thank you, Jesus.

Saint Mary Magdalene

Mary Magdalene was a disciple of Jesus. She was one of the women who went to the tomb. The women were the first ones to know that Jesus was raised from the dead. The Church celebrates her feast day on July 22.

Jesus Is Alive

After Jesus died on the cross, his friends buried his body in a tomb. Three days later some women who were disciples, or followers, of Jesus went to the place where Jesus was buried. The women were surprised at what they saw and heard. The Bible tells us,

When the women came to the tomb, they saw men in white robes. "Jesus is not here," the men said. "He has been raised from the dead. Go and tell the other disciples of Jesus."

BASED ON LUKE 24:1–4, 6; MATTHEW 28:7

The women did what they were told. They went to the other disciples. They told them that Jesus was raised from the dead. This is called the **Resurrection**.

Activity

Pretend you were with the women at the tomb of Jesus. What would you tell people? Share with your class.

Jesus Returned to His Father

After Jesus was raised from the dead, he stayed with his disciples for forty days. The Risen Jesus told his disciples to tell everyone in the world about him. Jesus told the disciples to invite everyone to believe in him and to be baptized.

Then Jesus returned to his Father in Heaven. We call this the Ascension. After we die, we hope that we too will return to God the Father in Heaven.

Activity

Listen to the story of Jesus' Ascension into Heaven. Act it out with your friends.

Catholics Believe

Candlemas Day

Each year the Church blesses candles on February 2. This day is called Candlemas Day. We use these candles in our churches and in our homes. They remind us of the Risen Jesus, the Light of the world. We, too, are to be lights in the world.

I Follow Jesus

The virtue of hope helps us to trust in God's love. When you tell others about Jesus, you are sharing God's love with people. You are a light in the world.

Activity

Jesus Is Alive!

Make a poster that tells people about Jesus. Use your poster as a reminder to act as a follower of Jesus.

My Faith Choice

This week I will share my poster. I will tell someone about Jesus. I will say:

_____

- -

_____

Pray, "Thank you, Jesus, for teaching me how to be a light in the world."

Chapter Review

Draw lines from the words in Column A to the sentences that they complete in Column B.

Column A

1. forgives

2. raised

3. cross

Column B

a. Jesus was _____ from the dead.

b. Jesus died on a _____ for all of us.

c. Jesus _____ us when we sin.

TO HELP YOU REMEMBER

1. Jesus loved us so much that he gave his life for us.

2. Jesus' rising from the dead is called his Resurrection.

3. Jesus returned to his Father in Heaven.

An Act of Hope

The Church gives us a special prayer called the Act of Hope. In this prayer, we tell God we always trust in his love for us. His word to us is always true. Pray this prayer together.

O my God,
you always love us.
You are always good to us.
You word to us is always true.
With your help, we hope that
we will live with you in Heaven.
Amen.

With My Family

This Week . . .

In chapter 6, "Jesus Shares God's Love," your child learned:

▶ Jesus showed his great love for us by dying on the cross.

▶ Three days after his death, Jesus was raised from the dead. Forty days later, Jesus ascended, or returned, to his Father in Heaven.

▶ Before he ascended to Heaven, Jesus commanded the disciples to evangelize the world. This means they were to tell all people about Jesus and his teaching. They were to make disciples of all people and to baptize them.

▶ Hope is the virtue that helps us remember and trust in God's love. We hope that one day we will live in happiness with God forever in Heaven.

For more about related teachings of the Church, see the *Catechism of the Catholic Church*, 561, 620–621, 629, 656–665, and the *United States Catholic Catechism for Adults*, pages 77–87.

■ Sharing God's Word

Read Luke 24:1–12, the account of the Resurrection. Or read the adaptation of the story on page 58. Emphasize that as the first disciples did, we are to tell people about Jesus.

■ We Live as Disciples

The Christian home and family is a school of discipleship. Choose one or more of the following activities to do as a family or design a similar activity of your own.

▶ Jesus tells us that we are to be lights in the world. Each night at dinner, light a candle as part of your mealtime prayer. Take turns telling about how each family member was a light in the world that day.

▶ It is difficult to know everyone in your parish. Each month make an effort to introduce yourselves as a family to one new family in your parish.

■ Our Spiritual Journey

Our spiritual pilgrimage is a journey of hope. It is with confidence that we trust that God's promise of eternal life will come true. Learn and help your child learn an act of hope. Pray it regularly.

For more ideas on ways your family can live as disciples of Jesus, visit

www.BeMyDisciples.com

CHAPTER 7

The Holy Spirit, Our Helper

? Who are some of the people who help you to learn new things?

Everyone needs teachers and helpers. The Holy Spirit is the special teacher and helper whom Jesus sent to us.

Jesus told his disciples, "God, my Father, will send you the Holy Spirit. The Holy Spirit will be your helper". BASED ON JOHN 14:26

? What do you know about the Holy Spirit?

Counsel

Counsel is another word for the help that a good teacher gives us. Counsel is a gift of the Holy Spirit. This gift helps us choose to live as followers of Jesus.

The Church Follows **Jesus**

Read to Me

Signs of the Holy Spirit

We can learn about God in many different ways, through words and pictures. Some churches have stained-glass windows. They may show Jesus, Mary, the saints, or symbols of the Holy Spirit. Flames of fire and a white dove are two symbols of the Holy Spirit.

The light shining through stained-glass windows reminds us of God's love for us. The Holy Spirit helps us to share that love with others.

Activity

Use the color key to color the stained-glass window. What symbols for the Holy Spirit do you see?

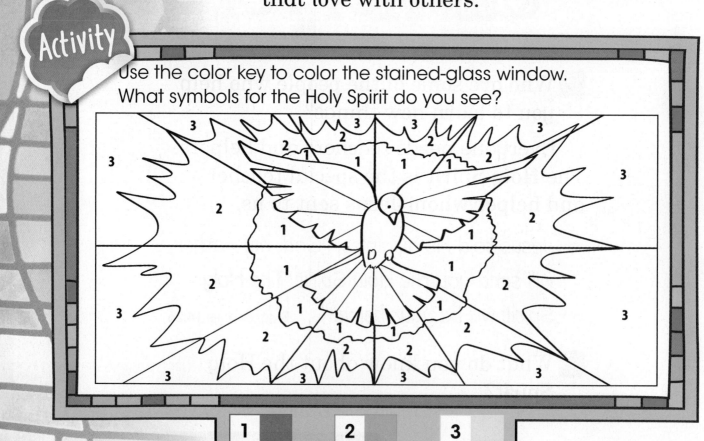

1   2   3

The Holy Spirit Is with Us

Jesus taught us that there is only one God. Jesus is the Son of God. He taught us about God the Father and God the **Holy Spirit**.

Jesus taught us that there is one God in Three Divine Persons. He taught that there is one God, who is God the Father, God the Son, and God the Holy Spirit. This is called the **Holy Trinity**.

Faith Focus
How does the Holy Spirit help and teach us?

Faith Words
Holy Spirit
The Holy Spirit is the Third Person of the Holy Trinity. The Holy Spirit is always with us to be our helper.

Holy Trinity
The Holy Trinity is one God in Three Divine Persons—God the Father, God the Son, and God the Holy Spirit.

Activity

A shamrock helps us remember that there are Three Divine Persons in one God. Trace the name of these Persons in the three Leaves.

Father

Son

Holy Spirit

Faith-Filled People

Saint Patrick

Saint Patrick was a bishop. He taught people in Ireland about the Holy Trinity. The Church celebrates the feast day of Saint Patrick on March 17.

Jesus' Promise

Jesus made a promise to his friends. He promised that God the Father would send them a helper. Jesus said,

The Father will give you a helper who will always be with you.

BASED ON JOHN 14:16

God the Holy Spirit is the helper whom the Father would send.

Jesus told his friends that the Holy Spirit would be their teacher and helper.

The Holy Spirit helps us understand what Jesus said and did. The Holy Spirit helps us live as Jesus' followers.

Activity

Color the spaces with **X**s one color and the spaces with **O**s other colors. Find out the name of the Third Person of the Holy Trinity.

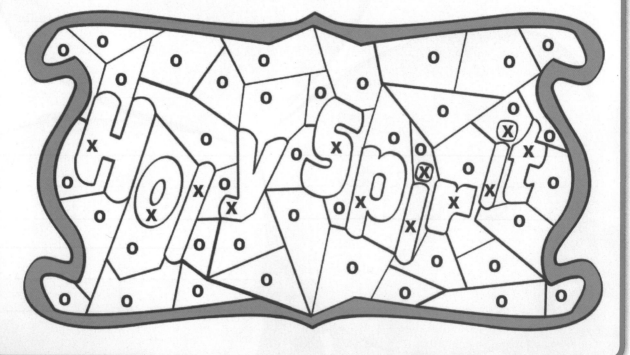

The Gift of the Holy Spirit

The Holy Spirit is the Third Person of the Holy Trinity. We first receive the gift of the Holy Spirit at Baptism. The Holy Spirit is always with us.

The Holy Spirit teaches us to pray. The Holy Spirit helps us learn what Jesus taught.

The Holy Spirit helps and teaches us to follow Jesus. Jesus told his followers,

Love one another as I love you.

BASED ON JOHN 13:34

The Holy Spirit helps and teaches us to love God and one another.

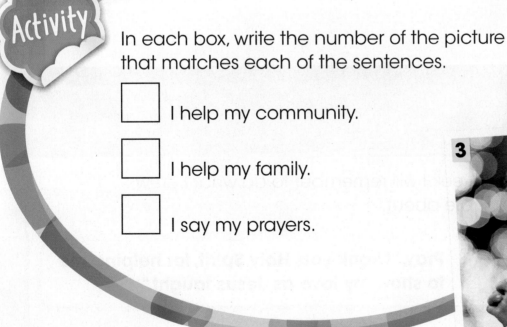

Activity

In each box, write the number of the picture that matches each of the sentences.

☐ I help my community.

☐ I help my family.

☐ I say my prayers.

I Follow Jesus

God the Holy Spirit is always with you. The Holy Spirit is your helper and teacher. The Holy Spirit helps you to make good choices as a follower of Jesus.

Activity

Teach Me to Love

Draw about the Holy Spirit helping you show love.

My Faith Choice

This week I will remember to do what I drew or wrote about.

Pray, "Thank you, Holy Spirit, for helping me to show my love as Jesus taught."

Chapter Review

Circle the names in the puzzle. Share what each name tells about God.

Father	Son	Holy Spirit

```
Q  (F  A  T  H  E  R)
W   S  O  N  E  O  P
H   O  L  Y  C  M  S
L   S  P  I  R  I  T
```

TO HELP YOU REMEMBER

1. The Holy Spirit helps and teaches us to pray.

2. The Holy Spirit helps us to know what Jesus taught.

3. The Holy Spirit helps and teaches us to do what Jesus asked us to do.

Come, Holy Spirit

Learn this prayer to the Holy Spirit.
Pray it together. Use gestures to pray.

Come,
Holy Spirit,
fill our hearts with
the fire of
your love.
Amen.

With My Family

This Week . . .

In chapter 7, "The Holy Spirit, Our Helper," your child learned:

▶ The Holy Trinity is the mystery of one God in Three Divine Persons. Before Jesus died, he promised the disciples that he would not leave them alone, and that the Father would send them the Advocate.

▶ The Holy Spirit is the Advocate whom the Father sent and who is always with us. The Holy Spirit helps us to know, believe, and live what Jesus taught.

▶ Counsel is a gift of the Holy Spirit that helps us to make good decisions, as Jesus taught.

For more about related teachings of the Church, see the *Catechism of the Catholic Church*, 232–248 and 683–741, and the *United States Catholic Catechism for Adults*, pages 101–110.

▪ Sharing God's Word

Read together the Gospel story in John 14:15–19. Emphasize that the Holy Spirit, the Advocate, is always with us to teach and help us to live as Jesus taught.

▪ We Live as Disciples

The Christian home and family is a school of discipleship. Choose one or more of the following activities to do as a family, or design a similar activity of your own.

▶ Make prayer cards, using the Prayer to the Holy Spirit on page 69. Decorate the cards with signs and symbols of the Holy Spirit. Keep the cards to remind you that the Holy Spirit is always with your family as teacher and helper.

▶ This week your child learned about the Holy Trinity. Now is a good time to review the Sign of the Cross with your child. Talk about how the Sign of the Cross names all three Persons of the Holy Trinity.

▪ Our Spiritual Journey

To give counsel is one of the Spiritual Works of Mercy. Make the Holy Spirit the center of your decision-making process and teach your child to do the same. Teach your child to respect the counsel of trusted adults, such as parents, teaches, and older family members. In this chapter, your child learned a prayer to the Holy Spirit. Read and pray together the prayer on page 69.

For more ideas on ways your family can live as disciples of Jesus, visit **www.BeMyDisciples.com**

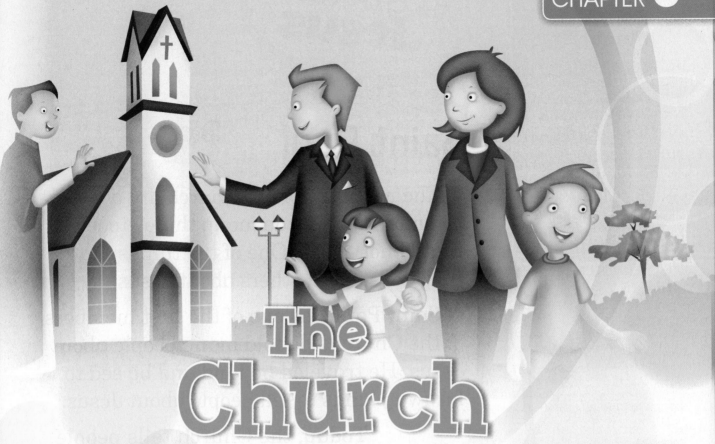

CHAPTER 8

The Church

❓ **What do you do together as a family?**

Each of us belongs to our family. We also belong to the family of the Church. The Bible tells us:

> The first members of the Church spent time together. They remembered Jesus. They shared all they had with one another. They prayed together. They broke and shared bread together. Together they praised God.

BASED ON ACTS OF THE APOSTLES 2:42

❓ **What does your family do at church?**

Reverence

The Holy Spirit gives us the gift of reverence. We show reverence to someone when we honor them and give them great respect.

The Church Follows Jesus

Saint Paul

Read to Me

The members of the Church are a community. They do many things together that honor Jesus. One of the things that they do is to tell others about Jesus.

Saint Paul was one of the first members of the Church. He told many people about Jesus. He traveled by land and by sea to faraway lands to tell people about Jesus.

Today, the Church tells people all over the world about Jesus Christ, just as Saint Paul did. We show reverence for Saint Paul and all holy people.

? Who do you know in the Church? How do they teach you and other people about Jesus?

Our Church Family

The People of God who believe in Jesus and live as his followers are called the **Church**.

After the Risen Jesus returned to his Father in Heaven, the disciples went to the city of Jerusalem. The Holy Spirit came to the them as Jesus had promised.

Read what happened:

The disciples were together in a room. The power of the Holy Spirit filled them. BASED ON ACTS OF THE APOSTLES 2:1–4

The Holy Spirit helped the disciples tell people about Jesus. They invited people to be baptized. The work of the Church began.

Faith Focus
Who helps us to live as followers of Jesus?

Faith Words
Church
The Church is the People of God who believe in Jesus and live as his followers.

Catholics
Catholics are followers of Jesus and members of the Catholic Church.

Activity Write or draw something Jesus did that you can share with others. Tell a partner. The Holy Spirit will help you.

Saint Peter the Apostle

Saint Peter the Apostle was one of the first disciples of Jesus. Jesus chose Peter to be the first leader of the whole Church. The Church celebrates the feast day of Saints Peter and Paul on June 29.

We Are Catholics

The Catholic Church goes all the way back to Jesus and the Apostles. We belong to the Catholic Church. We join the Catholic Church when we are baptized.

Catholics are followers of Jesus Christ. We do what Jesus taught us. We learn about God and his love for us. We teach others about Jesus. We work together to help others.

We pray together and share our love for Jesus.

Activity

Find the letter that goes with each number.
Write the letter on the line above the number.
Find out three things that Catholics do.

A	B	C	D	E	F	G	H	I	J	K	L	M
1	2	3	4	5	6	7	8	9	10	11	12	13

N	O	P	Q	R	S	T	U	V	W	X	Y	Z
14	15	16	17	18	19	20	21	22	23	24	25	26

L	E	A	R	N
12	5	1	18	14

16	18	1	25

8	5	12	16

The Saints

Members of the Church show us how to live as followers of Jesus. Some of these people are called saints. Saints are grown-ups and children from all over the world. They now live with God in Heaven. The Church has named many saints.

Mary, Mother of Jesus, is the greatest saint of all. We can pray to Mary and the other saints. All of the saints help us to l ive as children of God. They want us to live as followers of Jesus. They want us to be happy with God on Earth and in Heaven.

? Who shows you how to live as a child of God? How do they show you?

Holy Mary   Saint Joseph

Saint Joachim   Saint Anne

I Follow Jesus

The Holy Spirit gives you the gift of reverence. This gift helps you to honor God. You honor God when you serve him and others as Jesus taught. You show that you are a good Catholic.

Activity

Honoring God and Others

In one footstep, show how you will honor God. In the other footstep, show how you will honor others.

My Faith Choice

I can show reverence to God and others. This week I will do what I drew in the footsteps above.

Pray, "Thank you, God, for helping me to show that I belong to the Catholic Church."

Chapter Review

Color the circle next to the word that best complete each sentence.

1. The _____ came to Jesus' followers on Pentecost.
    - ○ Saints
    - ◉ Holy Spirit

2. _____ is the greatest saint.
    - ○ Peter
    - ○ Mary

3. Paul told many people about _____.
    - ○ Jesus
    - ○ Mary

▶ TO HELP YOU REMEMBER

1. The Holy Spirit helps all members of the Church.

2. The Church helps us to do what Jesus taught us.

3. The saints help us to live as followers of Jesus.

Litany of the Saints

We praise and thank God for the saints in a litany prayer. Pray together.

Leader   Holy Mary, Mother of God,

All   **pray for us.**

Leader   Saint Paul

All   **pray for us.**

Leader   Saint Anne, Mother to Mary,

All   **pray for us.**

Leader   All holy men and women,

All   **pray for us.**

With My Family

This Week . . .

In chapter 8, "The Church," your child learned:

▶ The Church began on Pentecost. On Pentecost, the Holy Spirit came upon the disciples, and they received the power to go out and preach to others about Jesus. The work that Jesus gave to the Church began.

▶ God has called us together in Christ to be his Church, the new People of God. Christ is the Head of the Church, the Body of Christ. We are members of the Church. We believe in Jesus Christ and in everything he revealed to us.

▶ We work together as the Body of Christ to share our love for Jesus with others. The saints provide us with examples of how to live as disciples of Jesus Christ in the world today.

▶ The Holy Spirit gives us the gift of reverence. This gift inspires us to honor God by serving him and others.

For more about related teachings of the Church, see the *Catechism of the Catholic Church*, 737–741 and 748–801, and the *United States Catholic Catechism for Adults*, pages 111–123.

■ Sharing God's Word

Read together the Bible story in Acts 2:1–41 about Pentecost or read the adaptation of the story on page 73. Emphasize that on Pentecost the Holy Spirit came to the disciples, and the disciples began the work of the Church.

■ We Live as Disciples

The Christian home and family is a school of discipleship. Choose one or more of the following activities to do as a family, or design a similar activity of your own.

▶ Identify and name ways that you live as members of the Catholic Church. For example, we take part in Mass, we help the poor and hungry, we help a neighbor in need, or we visit the sick.

▶ The saints show us how to live as followers of Jesus. If your parish is named after a saint, take time this week to find out more about the saint. Talk about how this saint or another saint, if your parish is not named after a saint, helps you live as a Christian family.

■ Our Spiritual Journey

The Church is the Communion of Saints. When we die, our life is changed but not ended. The saints of the Church continue to be our companions on our earthly journey. In this chapter, your child prayed part of the Litany of the Saints. Read and pray together the prayer on page 77.

For more ideas on ways your family can live as disciples of Jesus, visit **www.BeMyDisciples.com**

Unit 2 Review

A. Choose the Best Word

Complete the sentences. Color the circle next to the best choice.

1. God chose _____ to be the mother of Jesus.

   ◯ Gabriel   ◯ Mary

2. Jesus _____ us so much that he gave his life for us.

   ◯ loved   ◯ missed

3. Jesus returned to his Father in _____.

   ◯ Heaven   ◯ Nazareth

4. The _____ helps and teaches us to pray.

   ◯ Creator   ◯ Holy Spirit

5. The_____ of the Church help us to live as followers of Jesus.

   ◯ saints   ◯ angels

B. Show What You Know

Circle the numbers next to the words that tell about the Holy Trinity.

1. God the Father   **4.** the Holy Spirit

2. Mary, the Mother of God **5.** the People of God

3. Jesus the Son   **6.** the saints

C. Connect with Scripture

What was your favorite story about Jesus in this unit? Draw something that happened in the story. Tell your class about it.

D. Be a Disciple

1. *What saint or holy person did you enjoy hearing about in this unit? Write the name here. Tell your class what this person did to follow Jesus.*

_____

- -

_____

- -

_____

2. *What can you do to be a good disciple of Jesus?*

_____

- -

_____

- -

_____

We Worship
Part One

Come, Follow Me

Jesus looked out on the water and saw Simon and Andrew fishing. He called to them, "Come, follow me. I will teach you how to catch people, instead of fish."

The two brothers said, "Yes!" Off they went to follow Jesus.

Soon, Jesus spied two more fishermen named James and John. They were fixing their fishing nets.

"Come, follow me," Jesus said. The brothers said, "Yes!" Off they went to follow Jesus.

BASED ON MARK 1:16–20

What I Have Learned

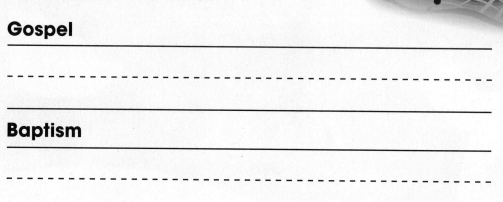

What is something you already know about these faith words?

Gospel

Baptism

Faith Words to Know

Put an **X** next to the faith words you know. Put a **?** next to the faith words you need to learn more about.

Faith Words

____ Easter   ____ modesty   ____ Marriage

____ Sacraments   ____ goodness

A Question I Have

What question would you like to ask about the Sacraments?

CHAPTER 9

The Church Celebrates Jesus

? What is your favorite season, or time, of the year?

The Church has seasons too. Let us listen to what the Bible tells us about the seasons of the year. In the Bible, God tells us:

> There is a season for everything. There is a time of the year for everything.

BASED ON ECCLESIASTES 3:1

? What is your favorite time of the year that you celebrate with the Church?

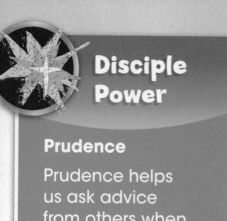
Prudence

Prudence helps us ask advice from others when making important decisions. A prudent person makes good choices. Our Church family helps us to make good choices.

The Church Follows **Jesus**

Celebrating Sunday

Sunday is the Lord's Day. Maya Lopez and her family keep Sunday holy in many ways.

Maya and her family gather with their Church family to worship God at Mass. Every Sunday they remember that Jesus was raised from the dead.

Sunday is a special family day too. Maya's family spends time together. Sometimes they visit relatives. Sometimes they gather for a special dinner. They celebrate that their family is part of God's family.

❓ How does your family celebrate Sunday as the Lord's Day?

The Seasons of the Church's Year

The different times of the **Church's year** are called its seasons. Each season of the Church's year tells us something about Jesus. All year long we remember God's love for us.

Advent, Christmas, Lent, Easter, and Ordinary Time are the seasons and time of the Church's year. Each season of the Church's year has its own color. This helps us to remember the season of the Church's year we are celebrating.

Advent

Advent is the first season of the Church's year. The Advent season is four weeks long. The Advent wreath reminds us to prepare for Christmas. We get our hearts ready for Jesus. The color for Advent is purple.

Faith Focus
What is the Church's year?

Faith Words
Church's year
The Church's year is made up of four seasons. They are Advent, Christmas, Lent, and Easter.

Easter
Easter is a season of the Church's year. It is the time of the year when we celebrate that Jesus was raised from the dead.

Activity

Color three candles purple and one candle pink in the Advent wreath. Tell how your parish or your family uses an Advent wreath to celebrate Advent.

Faith-Filled People

Saint Joseph

Saint Joseph was the husband of Mary and the foster father of Jesus. An angel told Joseph that Mary was going to have a baby. An angel told Mary and Joseph to give the baby the name Jesus. The Church celebrates the feast day of Saint Joseph on March 19.

Christmas

Christmas comes after Advent. During the Christmas season we remember the birth of Jesus. He is God's Son who came to live on Earth with us. Jesus is God's greatest gift to us.

The Church's celebration of Christmas is not just one day. The season of Christmas lasts two or three weeks. We use the color white to celebrate Christmas.

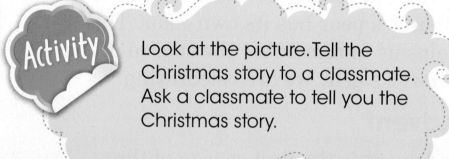

Activity

Look at the picture. Tell the Christmas story to a classmate. Ask a classmate to tell you the Christmas story.

Lent

During Lent we remember that Jesus died for us on the cross. We also get ready for Easter. The season of Lent begins on Ash Wednesday and lasts forty days. The color for Lent is purple.

Easter

During **Easter** we celebrate that Jesus was raised from the dead. This is the most important time of the Church's year. The season of Easter lasts about seven weeks. The Easter candle is lighted to remind us that Jesus is risen. The color for Easter is white.

Ordinary Time

During Ordinary Time we listen to Bible stories about what Jesus said and did. We learn to be followers of Jesus. The color for Ordinary Time is green.

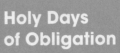
 **Activity** Color the symbols for Lent, Easter, and Ordinary Time. Use the colors of the seasons.

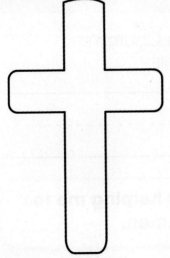

I Follow Jesus

When you celebrate the Church's seasons, you are making a good choice. Prudence helps you to make that good choice and others too.

Activity

Celebrating Jesus All Year

Look at the picture. Which season of the Church does it show?

_____

- - - - - - - - - - - - - - - - - -

_____

My Faith Choice

I will celebrate the season of the Church's year that we are in right now. I will

_____

- -

_____.

Pray, "Thank you, Holy Spirit, for helping me to celebrate the Church's year." Amen.

Chapter Review

Draw lines to match the Church seasons with what we celebrate.

Season	What We Celebrate
1. Easter	We get ready for Easter.
2. Christmas	We celebrate that Jesus was raised from the dead.
3. Lent	We get ready for Christmas.
4. Advent	We remember the birth of Jesus.

► **TO HELP YOU REMEMBER**

1. The Church has special times and seasons of the year.

2. The Church's year is made up of Advent, Christmas, Lent, Easter, and Ordinary Time.

3. Sunday is the Lord's Day.

Lord, We Praise You

When we worship God, we tell him that only he is God. Pray this prayer of praise together.

Jesus taught us to praise God.

Lord, we praise you.

In the morning and the night,

Lord, we praise you.

In the summer and the fall,

Lord, we praise you.

In the winter and the spring

Lord, we praise you.

With My Family

This Week . . .

In chapter 9, "The Church Celebrates Jesus," your child learned.

▶ The Church's year has special seasons just as the calendar year has. The seasons and time of the Church's year are Advent, Christmas, Lent, Easter, and Ordinary Time.

▶ Sunday is the Lord's Day.

▶ During the Church's year we join with Christ all year long and share in his work of Salvation. All year long we give thanks and praise to God.

▶ The virtue of prudence helps us to consistently make good choices. This includes taking part in Mass on Sunday.

For more about related teachings of the Church, see the *Catechism of the Catholic Church*, 1163–1173, and the *United States Catholic Catechism for Adults*, pages 173, 175, 178.

■ Sharing God's Word

Read together Psalm 150. Emphasize that throughout the liturgical year, the Church gives praise and thanksgiving to God. Talk about the ways in which your family is already giving thanks and praise to God.

■ We Live as Disciples

The Christian home and family is a school of discipleship. Choose one or more of the following activities to do as a family, or design a similar activity of your own.

▶ When you take part in Mass this week, look around and listen for all the signs that tell you what season of the Church year the Church is now celebrating. Point them out to your child and talk about them with her or him.

▶ Choose an activity that helps you celebrate the current liturgical season as a family at home. For example, during Advent you can use an Advent calendar to help anticipate and prepare for Christmas.

■ Our Spiritual Journey

Praising God is one of the five main forms of prayer that are part of the Church's tradition. In this chapter, your child prayed a prayer of praise on page 89. Pray this version of a prayer of praise as a family.

For more ideas on ways your family can live as disciples of Jesus, visit **www.BeMyDisciples.com**

CHAPTER 10

Signs of God's Love

? What special days and times does your family celebrate?

One time Jesus took part in a special celebration. John the Baptist baptized Jesus in the Jordan River.

As Jesus came up out of the water, he saw the clouds disappear. The Holy Spirit, like a dove, came down upon him.

A voice from the sky said, "You are my Son, the One I love." BASED ON MARK 1:10–11

? Why does God the Father love Jesus so much?

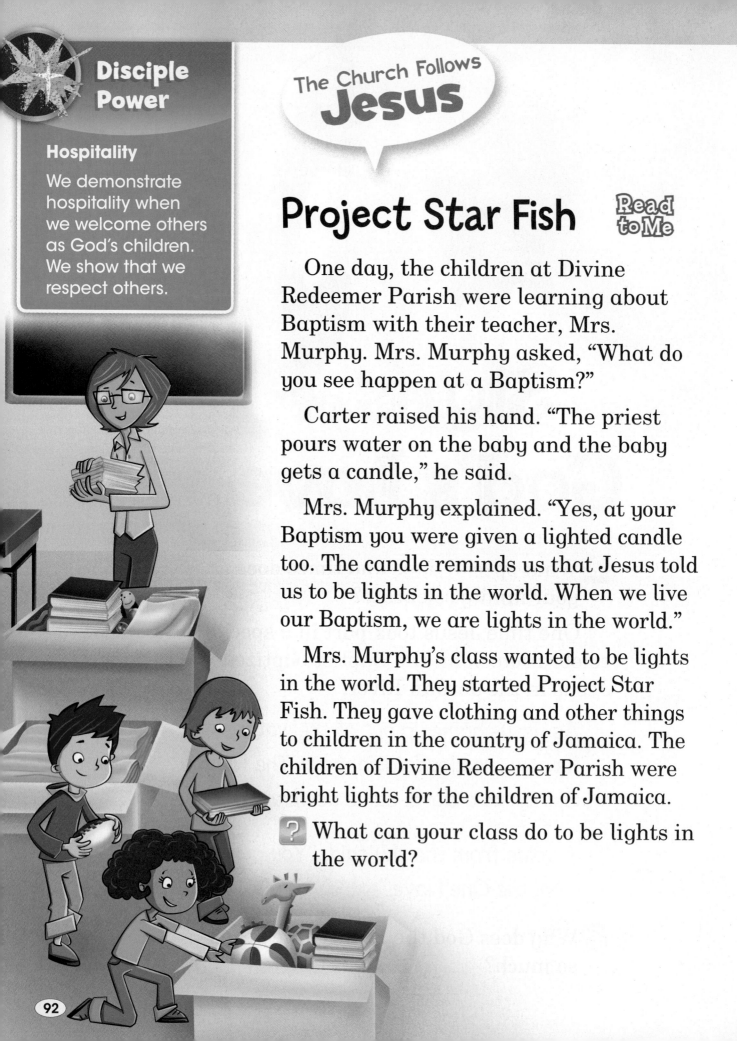

Hospitality

We demonstrate hospitality when we welcome others as God's children. We show that we respect others.

The Church Follows **Jesus**

Project Star Fish

Read to Me

One day, the children at Divine Redeemer Parish were learning about Baptism with their teacher, Mrs. Murphy. Mrs. Murphy asked, "What do you see happen at a Baptism?"

Carter raised his hand. "The priest pours water on the baby and the baby gets a candle," he said.

Mrs. Murphy explained. "Yes, at your Baptism you were given a lighted candle too. The candle reminds us that Jesus told us to be lights in the world. When we live our Baptism, we are lights in the world."

Mrs. Murphy's class wanted to be lights in the world. They started Project Star Fish. They gave clothing and other things to children in the country of Jamaica. The children of Divine Redeemer Parish were bright lights for the children of Jamaica.

❓ What can your class do to be lights in the world?

God Is with Us

Jesus gave the Church seven special signs and celebrations of God's love. We call these celebrations **sacraments**. The Seven Sacraments celebrate that God is with us. They are:

Baptism

Confirmation

Eucharist

Reconciliation

Anointing of the Sick

Holy Orders

Matrimony

In the Seven Sacraments, God shares his love and life with us. Each of the sacraments helps us to grow closer to God.

Faith Focus
What do we celebrate at Baptism and Confirmation?

Faith Words
sacraments
The sacraments are the seven signs and celebrations of God's love that Jesus gave the Church.

Baptism
Baptism is the first sacrament that we celebrate. In Baptism, we receive the gift of God's life and become members of the Church.

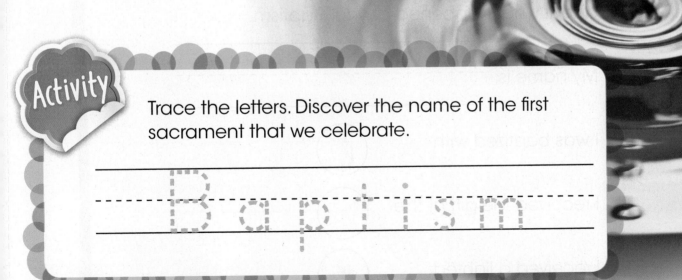

Activity

Trace the letters. Discover the name of the first sacrament that we celebrate.

Baptism

Godparents

Godparents help us to grow in faith. They show us how to love God and other people as Jesus taught.

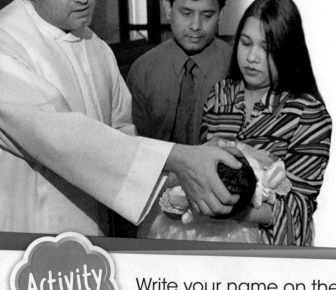

We Celebrate Baptism

Baptism is the first sacrament that we celebrate. We become members of the Church.

The priest or deacon pours water on our heads or puts us in the water three times. As he does this, he says, "I baptize you in the name of the Father, and of the Son, and of the Holy Spirit. Amen."

The pouring of water and the saying of the words tell us we receive the gift of God's life in Baptism. We receive the gift of the Holy Spirit.

Original Sin and any other sins that we have committed are forgiven. Original Sin is the first sin committed by Adam and Eve. We are born with this sin.

Activity

Write your name on the line. Read about what happened at your Baptism.

_____

My name is -

_____ .

I was baptized with .

I received the gift of the .

I received a lighted .

We Celebrate Confirmation

We celebrate Confirmation after we are baptized. Sometimes, we celebrate Confirmation right after Baptism, on the same day. If we celebrate Baptism when we are infants, we usually celebrate Confirmation when we are older.

At Confirmation, the bishop, or the priest named by the bishop, leads the celebration of Confirmation. During the celebration, he rubs special oil on the front of our heads. The oil is called Sacred Chrism. As he rubs the Chrism, he says, "Be sealed with the gift of the Holy Spirit."

The bishop or priest then says, "Peace be with you." We respond, "And also with you." The Holy Spirit teaches and helps us to live our Baptism. He helps us live as followers of Jesus. He teaches and helps us to be lights in the world.

Activity

Finish this prayer to the Holy Spirit.

Holy Spirit, help me to

_____

- -

_____

_____

- -

_____. Amen.

I Follow Jesus

At your Baptism, you became a member of the Church. At Confirmation, the Holy Spirit will give you special help to be a light in the world and welcome others.

Activity

Lights in the World

Draw one way you can be God's light in the world at home, at school, or in your neighborhood.

My Faith Choice

I want to be a light in the world. This week, I will:

_____

_____

Pray, "Thank you, Holy Spirit, for helping me to live as a follower of Jesus. Amen."

Chapter Review

Complete the sentences. Color the O next to the best choice.

1. There are _____ Sacraments.

    O three   O seven

2. _____ gave the Church the Sacraments.

    O Jesus   O The saints

3. _____ is the first sacrament that we receive.

    O Eucharist   O Baptism

Thank You, Lord

Pray this thank you prayer.

Leader   Let us thank God for the gift of water.

All   **Thank you, Lord.**

Leader   In Baptism, water is a sign that we receive the gift of God's life.

All   **Thank you, Lord..**

Leader   Come and dip your fingers in the water. Make the Sign of the Cross.

All   **Amen!**

TO HELP YOU REMEMBER

1. In Baptism, God shares his love and life with us.

2. In Baptism, we receive the gift of the Holy Spirit.

3. In Confirmation, we are sealed with the gift of the Holy Spirit to help us to live our Baptism.

With My Family

This Week . . .

In chapter 10, "Signs of God's Love," your child learned:

▶ Baptism is the first sacrament we receive.

▶ Through Baptism God makes us sharers in his life and love. We are reborn as children of God and receive the gift of the Holy Spirit. Original Sin and personal sins are forgiven. We become members of the Church, the Body of Christ.

▶ Confirmation strengthens the graces of Baptism.

▶ Hospitality is welcoming others as children of God. We show that we respect others.

For more about related teachings of the Church, see the *Catechism of the Catholic Church*, 1113–1130, and 1210–1274, and the *United States Catholic Catechism for Adults*, pages 183–197 and 203–209.

■ Sharing God's Word

Read together Matthew 5:14–16. Emphasize that at Baptism we are joined to Jesus, the Light of the world. Talk about how your family members are living their Baptism and are lights in the world.

■ We Live as Disciples

The Christian home and family is a school of discipleship. Choose one or more of the following activities to do as a family, or design a similar activity of your own.

▶ Make thank-you cards for godparents. Thank your godparents for helping you grow in faith.

▶ Sign your child on her or his forehead with a small sign of the cross before your child leaves for school. Remind your children that they are to be lights in the world.

■ Our Spiritual Journey

Baptism is the doorway to the Christian life. The ritual of blessing ourselves with holy water reminds us of our Baptism. Integrate the use of this ritual into your daily life. Perhaps, begin your family prayers by inviting everyone to bless themselves with holy water while praying the Sign of the Cross.

For more ideas on ways your family can live as disciples of Jesus, visit **www.BeMyDisciples.com**

CHAPTER 11

We Follow Jesus

? What good news have you heard this week?

Followers of Jesus have the best good news to share. Listen to what Jesus tells about sharing that good news:

Jesus would soon return to his Father in Heaven. He told his disciples "Go into the whole world. Tell everyone the good news I shared with you."

BASED ON MARK 16:15

? Who has shared the Good News of Jesus with you?

Goodness

Goodness is a sign that we are living our Baptism. When we are good to people, we show them that they are children of God. When we are good to people, we honor God.

The Church Follows **Jesus**

Read to Me

Saint Francis of Assisi

God's love filled the heart of Francis. So he sang about the Good News of Jesus.

Everywhere Francis went he told everyone about Jesus. He shared with everyone how much God loved them. He told people that God loves us so much that he gave us Jesus.

Everything good that Francis saw reminded him of how much God loves us. Today we honor Francis as a saint.

? What good thing in God's creation reminds you of God's love?

The Good News of Jesus

Faith Focus
Why do we share the Gospel with others?

Faith Word
Gospel
The Gospel is the Good News that Jesus told us about God's love.

Jesus told everyone the Good News of God's love. Jesus chose followers to help him share this Good News with all people. Disciples share the Good News of Jesus.

Jesus chose Matthew to be one of his first disciples. Matthew was one of the Apostles. Matthew wrote about the Good News of Jesus. He wrote the Good News about Jesus in his **Gospel**. The word gospel means "good news."

 **Activity**

Color the s next to the ways you can share the Good News of God's love.

 Tell people about Jesus.

 Say "Thank you" to someone who is kind to me.

Make a get-well card for a friend who is sick.

 Be rude to someone who is not kind to me.

Blessed Teresa of Calcutta

Mother Teresa was born in the country of Albania. When she was in high school, she knew God was calling her to serve the poorest of the poor. She founded the Missionaries of Charity to help her do that work. Today, Missionaries of Charity share the Good News of God's love with poor, sick, and dying people around the world.

Tell the Good News

The last story in Matthew's Gospel tells about Jesus returning to his Father in Heaven. In this story, we hear the important work that Jesus gave to his disciples:

> Jesus told his disciples, "Go to every land you can. Invite all people to be my disciples. Baptize them in the name of the Father, and of the Son, and of the Holy Spirit. Teach them what I have taught you."

BASED ON MATTHEW 28:19–20

? How do Christians today tell others about the Good News?

Followers of Jesus Christ

The disciples of Jesus traveled to small villages and to large cities. They walked. They rode donkeys. They traveled in ships.

They did the work that Jesus had given them to do. They told everyone the Good News of Jesus Christ. They baptized people. Many people became followers of Jesus Christ. People called the followers of Jesus Christians.

When we hear the Gospel, we come to know Jesus better. We grow in faith. We grow in our love for God, for ourselves, and for other people.

Activity

Trace the way to Jesus. Find and circle the things that followers of Jesus share with others.

Love

Peace

Joy

Goodness

Forgiveness

I Follow Jesus

You can be a disciple of Jesus. There are many good ways to tell others about Jesus. The Holy Spirit helps you to tell people about the Good News of Jesus.

Tell the Good News

Imagine that you are one of the children in the picture. Write what you want to tell other people about Jesus.

My Faith Choice

Check (√) what you will do this week. I will share what I have written about Jesus with

- ☐ my parents
- ☐ a friend
- ☐ my grandparents
- ☐ someone at church

 Pray, Tell the Holy Spirit what you have decided to do. In your own words, ask him to help you.

Chapter Review

*Remember the name for Jesus' Good News. Color the spaces with **X**s red. Color the spaces with **Y**s another color.*

▶ TO HELP YOU REMEMBER

1. The Gospel is the Good News that Jesus told about God's love.

2. Jesus told his disciples to tell everyone the Good News that he shared with them.

3. When we listen to the Gospel, we come to know Jesus better and to grow in faith.

Lord, Help Us to Listen

At Mass, we pray silently before we listen to the Gospel. We trace a small cross on our foreheads, on our lips, and over our hearts. Learn to pray in this new way.

Jesus, be in my thoughts,

on my lips,

and in my heart. Amen.

With My Family

This Week . . .

In chapter 11, "We Follow Jesus," your child learned:

▶ The Gospel is the Good News about Jesus. Matthew, Mark, Luke, and John are the four gospel writers.

▶ The last story in Matthew's Gospel is about Jesus telling his disciples to preach the Gospel and to baptize people.

▶ Christians are to treat people with goodness. Goodness is a fruit of the Holy Spirit. It is a sign we know that every person is a child of God. In doing so, we are cooperating with the graces we received at Baptism.

For more about related teachings of the Church, see the *Catechism of the Catholic Church*, 124–133 and 849–856, and the *United States Catholic Catechism for Adults*, pages 79–85.

■ Sharing God's Word

Read together Matthew 28:19–20, the story about the commissioning Jesus' disciples. Or read the adaptation of the story on page 102. Emphasize that Jesus told the disciples to invite all people to be his disciples. Talk about how your family shares the Gospel with others.

■ We Live as Disciples

The Christian home and family is a school of discipleship. Choose one or more of the following activities to do as a family, or design a similar activity of your own.

▶ Saint Francis of Assisi sang about the Good News of Jesus. Invite each family member to share their favorite song or hymn that tells about Jesus. Be sure that everyone explains why the song or hymn is their favorite.

▶ Invite family members to share one thing that they would like everyone in the family to know about Jesus.

■ Our Spiritual Journey

When we are good to people, we show them respect as children of God. We are a sign to them of how much God loves them. We grow in respect for ourselves. We are all children of God. Practice the prayer form on page 105 with your child. Remind them that we say these words silently when the priest introduces the Gospel at Mass.

For more ideas on ways your family can live as disciples of Jesus, visit **www.BeMyDisciples.com**

CHAPTER 12

The Catholic Family

? Who belongs to your family?

Like you, Jesus grew up in a family. Listen to what the Bible tells us about Jesus' family:

> When Jesus was a baby, Mary and Joseph presented him to the Lord in the Temple in Jerusalem. When they returned to the family home in Nazareth, Jesus grew up there. He came to know what God wanted him to do.
>
> BASED ON LUKE 2:22, 39–40

? What do these words from the Bible tell you about Jesus' family?

Disciple Power

Fidelity

Being faithful means to keep our promises. Parents show fidelity when they love and care for their children.

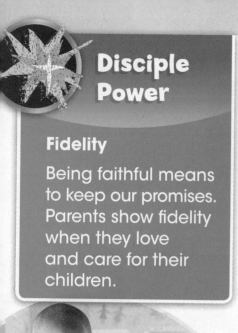

Helping Families

In Landon's family, both parents need to work to provide food, clothes, and many other things that a family needs.

Holy Family Day Home was started by the Sisters of the Holy Family. It is a place for children to stay while both of their parents work.

Landon's parents saw that the Holy Family Day Home was a safe place for Landon to be after school when they were at work. The children learn to respect themselves and others. Landon and the other children play and learn after school.

Holy Family Day Home helps parents care for their children.

? What are some things you enjoy doing after school?

The Gift of Marriage

When a man and a woman love each other very much, they marry each other. They make a promise to love each other and live as a family their whole lives.

The Gospel of John tells us about a **marriage**:

Jesus and Mary, his mother, and the disciples went to a wedding. During the party, the married couple ran out of wine. Jesus blessed six large jars of water, and the water became wine. Jesus gave the wine to the married couple.

BASED IN JOHN 2:1–11

Activity

Look at the pictures of the families on this page. Draw a picture of your family.

Saint Elizabeth Ann Seton

Elizabeth Ann Seton was the first person born in the United States who was named a saint. Elizabeth and her husband, William, were the parents of five children. They showed God's love to each other and to their children.

Families Are Signs of God's Love

When Catholics get married, they celebrate the Sacrament of **Matrimony**. A husband and a wife sometimes receive the wonderful gift of children from God. They become parents.

There are many different kinds of families. All families are called to love God and one another. Families are to be signs of God's love in their homes and in the world.

A family is a blessing from God. Members of a family share their love with God and with one another. They pray together. They respect one another. They say and do kind things for one another. They take care of one another. They honor and respect each other as children of God.

Activity

Write your family name. Tell your class how your family is a sign of God's love.

_____

- -

_____

The Family of God

At Baptism, we become part of God's family, the Church. Our Church family helps us to grow as Catholics.

The Church teaches us about the Holy Family. Mary, Joseph, and Jesus are the Holy Family.

Our family is the church of the home. Our family helps us to grow in faith. It helps us to live our faith. It teaches us to pray and to care for others as Jesus did.

Catholics Believe

The Family Church

Our families help us to know and love Jesus. They help us to live as disciples of Jesus. That is why we call our family "the family Church" or "the church of the home."

Activity

Check (√) the ways that your family can help you grow in faith and live as a child of God.

- ☐ Pray as a family each day.
- ☐ Read the Bible together.
- ☐ Go to Mass.
- ☐ Share one other thing that your family can do:

_____

_____

_____

I Follow Jesus

You are part of your family. You are part of God's family, the Church. God the Holy Spirit helps you to love your family. When you do this, you honor and respect your parents and the other members of your family.

Activity

Sharing Family Love

Learn to sign these words. Teach the signs to your family. Share God's love with one another.

God

loves

you.

My Faith Choice

This week I will share God's love with a member of my family. I will sign the message, "God loves you," for them.

 Pray, "Thank you, Holy Spirit, for helping me to share God's love with my family. Amen."

Chapter Review

Read this poem. Fill in the blanks with rhyming words.

1. Families, families, everywhere _____

    -

    show each other love and _____.

2. They tell us of God's love, you see. _____

    -

    God loves each of us, you and _____.

TO HELP YOU REMEMBER

1. Christian families are signs of Jesus' love in the world.

2. Members of a family share their love for God with one another.

3. Our family helps us to live our faith.

A Family Blessing

Ask God to bless your family. Pray this prayer now with your classmates.

Leader   Lord God, show your wonderful love to all of our families.

Leader   Bless our parents and grandparents,

All   **we ask you, Lord.**

Leader   Bless (*say other names silently in your heart*),

All   **we ask you, Lord. Amen.**

With My Family

This Week . . .

In chapter 12, "The Catholic Family," your child learned:

▶ God invites a man and a woman to share their love for him and for one another forever in marriage.

▶ Matrimony is the sacrament that Catholics celebrate when they marry.

▶ The Christian family is the "Church of the home," or the "family Church."

▶ Families are signs of God's love. Families are the primary place where parents and children experience and grow in faith, hope, and love.

▶ Fidelity helps children and parents grow stronger as a family in their love for God and for one another. Fidelity helps us live the Fourth Commandment.

For more about related teachings of the Church, see the *Catechism of the Catholic Church*, 1601–1658 and 2197–2233, and the *United States Catholic Catechism for Adults*, pages 279–287.

Sharing God's Word

Read together Luke 2:41–52, the finding of the twelve-year-old Jesus in the Temple. Emphasize that in the Holy Family, Jesus grew in love for God and for his family. Talk about the things that your family does to help one another grow in love for God and for one another.

We Live as Disciples

The Christian home and family is a school of discipleship. Choose one or more of the following activities to do as a family, or design a similar activity of your own.

▶ When we pray as a family, we show that our family loves God. Make an extra effort this week to pray together as a family at least once a day.

▶ Talk about the many ways in which your family is a sign of God's love; for example, when you do kind things for one another, when you pray together, and so on. Encourage one another to continue doing these things.

Our Spiritual Journey

A blessing is a sacramental. Sacramentals are sacred signs given to us by the Church. We use blessings to dedicate things or special occasions or people to God. Read and pray the blessing prayer on page 113 together as a family.

For more ideas on ways your family can live as disciples of Jesus, visit **www.BeMyDisciples.com**

Unit 3 Review

A. Choose the Best Word

*Complete the sentences. Color the circle next
to the best choice.*

1. Advent, Christmas, Lent and _____
are all seasons of the Church year.

　　○ Winter　　　　○ Easter

2. Jesus gave the Church seven _____ to
help us grow closer to God.

　　○ Commandments　○ Sacraments

3. The first _____ of Jesus told everyone
the Good News of God's love.

　　○ family　　　　○ disciples

4. When we listen to the _____, we come
to know Jesus better and grow in faith.

　　○ Gospel　　　　○ music

5. Christian families are _____ of Jesus'
love for his followers.

　　○ signs　　　　○ homes

B. Show What You Know

*Use purple, green, or gold to color the circle
next to each season or time of the Church year.
Use the correct color for each season or time.*

　　○ Advent　　　　○ Ordinary Time

　　○ Easter　　　　○ Christmas

　　○ Lent

C. Connect with Scripture

What was your favorite story about Jesus in this unit? Draw something that happened in the story. Tell your class about it.

D. Be a Disciple

1. *What saint or holy person did you enjoy hearing about in this unit? Write the name here. Tell your class what this person did to follow Jesus.*

_____

- -

_____

- -

_____

2. *What can you do to be a good disciple of Jesus?*

_____

- -

_____

- -

_____

We Worship
Part Two

A Time to Celebrate

Once Jesus invited a man named Levi to follow him. Levi said, "Yes!" He was so happy that he gave a big party. But some people did not like Levi. They said to Jesus's disciples, "We are so mad! Jesus is at a party with sinners. That is very bad!"

But Jesus said, "Of course I am here with sinful people. I am here to forgive them and give them peace. When sinful people stop doing what is wrong and turn their hearts to God, it is the best time to celebrate."

BASED ON LUKE 5:27–32

What I Have Learned

What is something you already know about these faith words?

prayer

_____

- -

_____

Mass

_____

- -

_____

Faith Words to Know

Put an **X** next to the faith words you know.
Put a **?** next to the faith words you need
to learn more about.

Faith Words

| _____ patience | _____ Galilee | _____ wisdom |
| _____ Eucharist | _____ miracle | _____ Our Father |

A Question I Have

What question would you like to ask about
the Mass?

_____

- -

_____

CHAPTER 13

We Pray

? What are some of your favorite prayers?

Sometimes we pray for ourselves. Other times we pray for our family and friends. Jesus taught his followers how to pray. Listen to what Jesus said.

> You do not need to use many words when you talk to God. Talk to God from your heart. BASED ON MATTHEW 6:7

? What prayers do you pray with your Church family?

Disciple Power

Patience

We act with patience when we listen carefully to others. We pay attention when others are helping us.

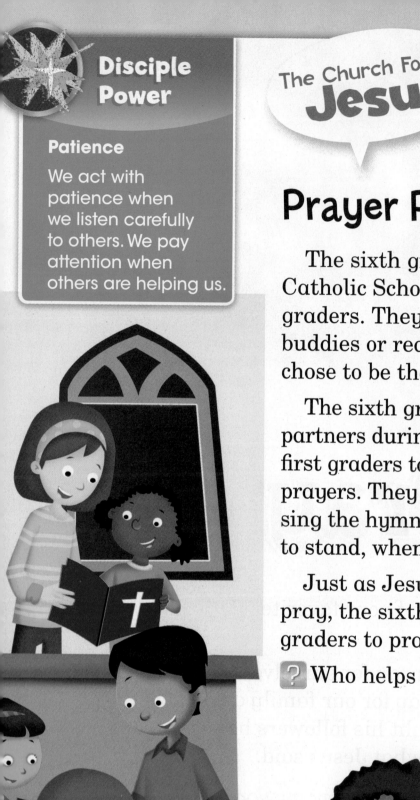

The Church Follows **Jesus**

Prayer Partners

Read to Me

The sixth graders at Holy Nativity Catholic School wanted to help the first graders. They considered being lunch buddies or reading friends. Finally, they chose to be their prayer partners.

The sixth graders sat with their prayer partners during Mass. They helped the first graders to learn the words to the prayers. They helped the first graders to sing the hymns. They taught them when to stand, when to sit, and when to kneel.

Just as Jesus taught his disciples to pray, the sixth graders helped the first graders to pray.

? Who helps you learn how to pray?

God Hears Our Prayers

Faith Focus
Why is it important to pray?

Faith Word
prayer
Prayer is listening and talking to God.

Friends and family members listen and talk to each other. We can share what is on our minds and in our hearts.

Prayer is listening and talking to God. We share with God what is on our minds and in our hearts.

We can pray anywhere and anytime. The Holy Spirit helps us to pray. When we pray, we grow in our love for God.

Activity

Trace this message. Tell a partner how you pray.

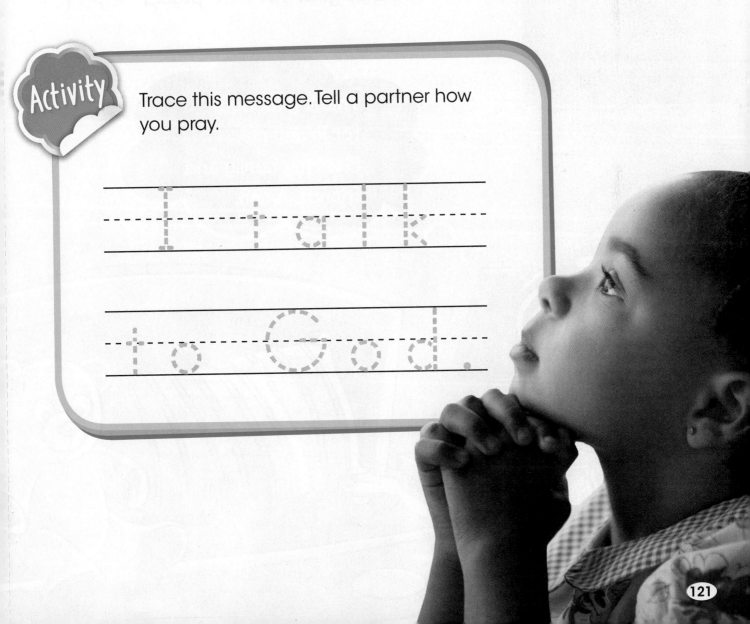

I talk
to God.

121

Faith-Filled People

Saint Thérèse, the Little Flower

Saint Thérèse of Lisieux is also called the Little Flower. Thérèse found a favorite place to pray. When she was young, she would pray in the space between her bed and the wall. The Church celebrates the feast day of Saint Thérèse, the Little Flower, on October 1.

Jesus Shows Us How to Pray

Jesus prayed all during his life. Jesus prayed alone. Sometimes he prayed with his family. Sometimes Jesus prayed with his friends. Other times Jesus prayed with his neighbors.

Sometimes we pray alone. Sometimes we pray with others. We pray with our family. We pray with our friends. We pray with our Church family.

? Where is your favorite place to pray? Why is it your favorite place?

Thank you, God, for loving me. Bless my family and friends. Amen.

God Always Listens

Jesus told us that God is our Father. God the Father invites us to talk with him in prayer. He wants us to share with him what is on our minds and in our hearts.

We do what Jesus taught us. We tell God the Father we love him. We thank him for his blessings.

We ask God to take care of us and our families. We ask God to help other people. We ask God to forgive us and to help us live as his children.

Activity

Look at the picture. Write a short prayer the child might be praying.

"God our loving Father,

_____

- -

_____

_____

- -

_____"

- -

_____

Amen.

I Follow Jesus

The Holy Spirit teaches you to pray. You can talk to God about anything. You can pray anywhere and anytime. Patience helps you pray. It helps you spend time with God.

Activity

Times to Pray

Fill in the chart. Name something or someone you can pray for at different times during the day.

Morning	
Afternoon	
Evening	

My Faith Choice

This week I will pray to be a patient person. I will pray in the morning, afternoon, and evening.

Pray, "Thank you, Holy Spirit, for helping me be patient with others. Amen."

Chapter Review

Color the circle ⬤ *if the sentence is true.*
Color the circle ⬤ *if the sentence is not true.*

	T	F
1. We can talk to God about anything.	○	○
2. We can talk to God anywhere.	○	○
3. We can pray only by ourselves.	○	○
4. Jesus prayed often.	○	○
5. God cannot hear our prayers.	○	○

TO HELP YOU REMEMBER

1. Prayer is listening and talking to God.

2. When we pray, we grow in our love for God.

3. God always listens to our prayers.

Hail, Mary

*Mary, the mother of Jesus, prays for us.
She helps us to pray. Learn these words
from the Hail Mary prayer. Pray them often.
Pray them alone and with your family.*

**Hail, Mary, full of grace,
the Lord is with thee.
Blessed art thou among women
and blessed is the fruit of thy
womb, Jesus.**

With My Family

This Week . . .

In chapter 13, "We Pray," your child learned:

▶ Prayer is listening and talking to God.

▶ Jesus is our example for how we are to pray.

▶ We can pray anywhere and anytime. We can share with God everything and anything that is on our minds and in our hearts.

▶ We demonstrate patience when we listen carefully to people and pay attention when they are helping us. Patience helps us to spend time with God in prayer, even when we want to do something else.

For more about related teachings of the Church, see the *Catechism of the Catholic Church*, 2558–2619; and the *United States Catholic Catechism for Adults*, pages 466–468 and 476–477.

■ Sharing God's Word

Read Matthew 7:7–11 together. Emphasize that prayer is listening and talking to God. We can pray anywhere and anytime. God knows what we need before we ask him.

■ We Live as Disciples

The Christian home and family is a school of discipleship. The first place where children should learn to live as disciples of Jesus. Choose one of the following activities to do as a family, or design a similar activity of your own.

▶ Go for a walk together. Thank God for everything you see and hear.

▶ **Family prayer time** helps us be aware that God is always with us. Evaluate your family prayer time. Do what it takes to integrate time for prayer into your family's daily activities and schedule.

■ Our Spiritual Journey

Mary is the first disciple of her son, Jesus. She is the model of what it means to be a disciple of Jesus. Devotion to Mary is beneficial to the life of Catholics. Incorporate frequent conversations with Mary. Seek direction for your life by meditating on the mysteries of the Rosary, the prayer devotion that Mary gave us.

For more ideas on ways your family can live as disciples of Jesus, visit

www.BeMyDisciples.com

CHAPTER 14

We Are Peacemakers

❓ Who has forgiven you?
Whom have you forgiven?

Forgiving others shows our love for one another. Christians forgive one another. Jesus tells us to forgive people who have hurt us. Jesus said,

> "Ask God to forgive your sins and to help you forgive those who have hurt you."
> BASED ON MATTHEW 6:12

❓ What did Jesus teach about forgiveness?

Disciple Power

Peace

We live as peacemakers when we forgive those who have hurt us. We ask for forgiveness when we have hurt others. These actions bring peace to us and to others.

The Church Follows Jesus

Read to Me

The Pope Makes Peace

Pope John Paul II was riding in the back of his car. He was greeting and waving to people.

A man came out of the crowd and shot at the pope. The pope was hurt but soon got better.

Later, Pope John Paul II went to the prison. He visited the man who shot him. He put his arms around the man and forgave him. The pope made peace with him. He showed us what Jesus wants us to do.

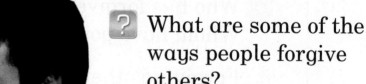 What are some of the ways people forgive others?

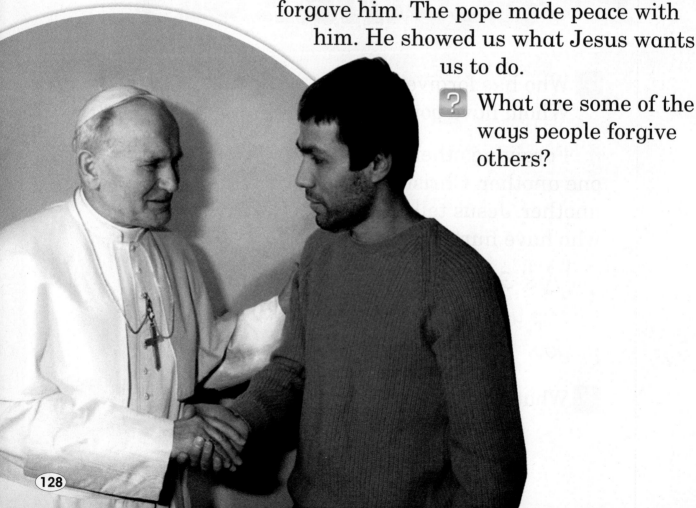

Making Peace

We can use words and actions to help others. Other times, we can choose to use our words and actions to hurt others. When we hurt others, we do not obey God. We **sin.**

Sin is choosing to do or say something that we know is against God's laws. When we sin, we turn away from God's love.

Sin is choosing not to love others as Jesus taught us. Sin hurts our friendship with God and with other people.

Faith Focus
Why is it important to say "I am sorry" when we choose to do or say something that is wrong?

Faith Word
sin
Sin is choosing to do or say something that we know is against God's laws.

Activity

Look at these pictures. Pretend you are making a movie. With a partner, act out a picture showing a good choice.

Asking for Forgiveness

We feel sorry when we sin. We want to be forgiven. We want to make up for our sin.

We need to say that we are sorry to people when we hurt them. We need to ask for forgiveness. We want everything to be right again.

We also need to tell God that we are sorry when we sin. We can tell God that we are sorry. We ask for forgiveness because we love God. God will always forgive us because he loves us.

Activity

Circle the words that show you are sorry. Also circle the words that show you forgive somone.

It's o.k.

I'm sorry.

It's my fault.

Go away.

Let's be friends.

Forgiving Others

Jesus tells us to forgive people who have hurt us. He tells us to forgive them over and over again.

Sometimes it is not easy to do what Jesus wants us to do. Sometimes we do not feel like forgiving people who have hurt us. The Holy Spirit can help us forgive others.

We open our hearts with love when we forgive others. We show our love for God and for one another. We are peacemakers.

? How do you show forgiveness? How do other people show you forgiveness?

Catholics Believe

Sign of Peace

Each Sunday at Mass, we shake hands or share another sign of peace with one another. This shows that we want to forgive those who have hurt us. We want to live together as the one family of God.

I Follow Jesus

The Holy Spirit teaches you and helps you forgive people. He also helps you to ask for forgiveness. When you forgive someone, you are a peacemaker.

Activity

A Forgiving Tree

In the leaves, write words or draw actions that show forgiveness.

My Faith Choice

This week I will use the forgiving words or actions that I wrote or drew in the activity. I will bring peace to others.

Pray, "Thank you, Holy Spirit, for teaching me and helping me to live as a peacemaker. Amen."

Chapter Review

Choose the best word and write it in the space in each sentence.

forgive	peace	sin

_____

- - - - - - - - - - - - - - - - - - - -

1. When we _____, we turn away from God's love.

_____

- - - - - - - - - - - - - - - - - - - -

2. Jesus asks us to _____ others.

_____

- - - - - - - - - - - - - - - - - - - -

3. We bring _____ when we show our love for others.

▶ TO HELP YOU REMEMBER

1. Sin hurts our friendship with God and others.

2. When we say that we are sorry, we show that we love God and others.

3. When we say that we are sorry, we ask for forgiveness from others and from God.

Prayer of Mercy

At the beginning of Mass, we ask God for his mercy. The word mercy reminds us that forgiveness is a gift of God's love. Pray this prayer together.

Leader Lord, have mercy.

All **Lord, have mercy.**

Leader Christ, have mercy.

All **Christ, have mercy.**

Leader Lord, have mercy.

All **Lord, have mercy. Amen.**

With My Family

This Week . . .

In chapter 14, "We Are Peacemakers," your child learned:

▶ People make choices that help others or hurt others. We can choose to follow or reject God's laws.

▶ People can sin. Sin always hurts our relationship with God and with others. When we sin, we need to say that we are sorry both to God and to those whom we have hurt. We need to ask for forgiveness. We need to reconcile our relationships with God and with people.

▶ We live as peacemakers when we are honest in our relationships and with God. When we forgive others, we are peacemakers.

For more about related teachings of the Church, see the *Catechism of the Catholic Church*, 1420–1484 and 1846–1869; and the *United States Catholic Catechism for Adults*, pages 235–236.

■ Sharing God's Word

Read together the Bible story in Matthew 18:21–35 about the Parable of the Unforgiving Servant. Emphasize that Jesus teaches us that we are to forgive others over and over again, as God always forgives us when we are truly sorry for our sins.

■ We Live as Disciples

The Christian home and family is a school of discipleship. Choose one of the following activities to do as a family, or design a similar activity of your own.

▶ When you participate in Mass this week, pay close attention to the prayer of mercy that we pray at the beginning. Remember that the word *mercy* reminds us that God's forgiveness is a gift of his love.

▶ Name ways that people show that they are sorry. Talk about ways that members of your family can show both forgiveness to one another and accept forgiveness from one another.

■ Our Spiritual Journey

In this chapter, your child prayed a prayer of mercy. This is one of the three forms of prayer that the Church uses for the Penitential Act in the Introductory Rites of the Mass. Through this prayer, we are reconciled with God and one another. We enter into the celebration of the Eucharist in the right relationship with God and one another, as peacemakers. Read and pray together the prayer on page 133.

For more ideas on ways your family can live as disciples of Jesus, visit

www.BeMyDisciples.com

CHAPTER 15

We Go to Mass

? When do you say thank you to others?

We can thank people in many ways. The Church thanks God in a special way at Mass. Listen to what the Bible tells us about giving thanks to God.

It is good to give thanks to God.

BASED ON PSALMS 92:2

? When do you say thank you to God?

Disciple Power

Perseverance

Perseverance helps us to live our faith when it is difficult. We do not give up even when it is not easy to do something good.

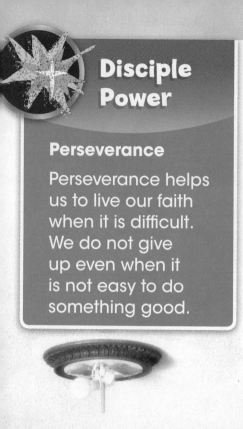

Sharing God's Love

First Holy Communion was a special day for Peyton and the other children of St. Mary's Church. At the end of Mass, they heard Father Julio say, "Go in peace, glorifying the Lord by your life."

At the next religion class, Peyton asked Mrs. Hensle, "What did Father Julio tell us to do? I don't understand."

Mrs. Hensle explained, "Father Julio said we need to show we are children of God by what we say and do." The children talked about what they could do.

They visited elderly people living in a retirement home. They played a board game together. This was their way of saying thank you for the gift of First Holy Communion. They shared God's love with other people.

? How can you share God's love with people?

We Gather at Mass

The **Mass** is the most important celebration of the Church. We gather as the People of God. We give glory to God. We show that we love and honor God.

We listen to God's Word. We celebrate and share in the **Eucharist.** The Eucharist is the sacrament in which we receive the Body and Blood of Christ.

We begin the Mass by praying the Sign of the Cross. This reminds us of our Baptism. We remember that we belong to Jesus and are members of the Church.

Faith Focus
Why does our Church family gather to celebrate Mass?

Faith Words

Mass
The Mass is the most important celebration of the Church.

Eucharist
The Eucharist is the sacrament in which we receive the Body and Blood of Christ.

Activity

Draw you and your family at Mass.

Faith-Filled People

Priests

Priests are the Bishop's co-workers. They lead us in the celebration of the Mass. They teach us what Jesus taught. They help us to live as followers of Jesus.

We Listen to God's Word

We listen to readings from the Bible at every Mass. God tells us about his love for us. On Sunday we listen to three readings. The third reading is from the Gospel.

After the Gospel is read, the priest or deacon helps us to understand God's Word. We come to know and love God more. We learn ways to live as Jesus taught.

Next, we tell God that we have listened to his Word. We tell God we believe in him. Then we pray for other people and for ourselves.

Activity

Learn what we say after the First Reading at Mass. Trace these words.

Thanks

be to

God.

We Give Thanks to God

At Mass we celebrate the Eucharist. The word eucharist means "to give thanks."

In the celebration of the Eucharist, we give thanks to God. We remember and do what Jesus did at the Last Supper.

The Last Supper is the meal that Jesus ate with his disciples on the night before he died.

At the Last Supper Jesus took bread and wine. He took the bread and said, "This is my body." He took the cup of wine and said, "This is my blood."

BASED ON MATTHEW 26:26–28

Activity

Color the letters. Tell others what we do at Mass.

WE GIVE THANKS TO GOD.

I Follow Jesus

At Mass you can listen to God's Word. You learn ways to live as a follower of Jesus. In the celebration of the Eucharist, you give thanks to God. You can try to pay attention at Mass, even when it is hard.

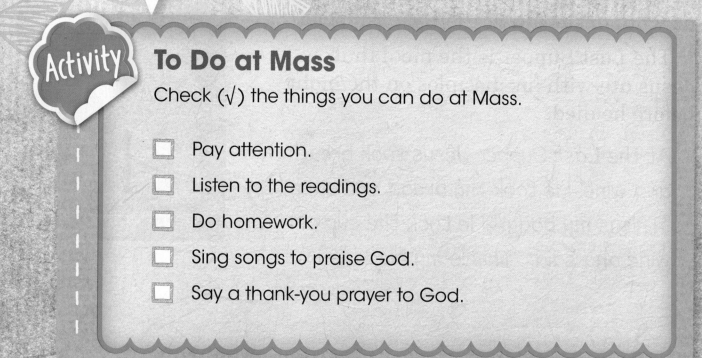

Activity

To Do at Mass

Check (√) the things you can do at Mass.

- ☐ Pay attention.
- ☐ Listen to the readings.
- ☐ Do homework.
- ☐ Sing songs to praise God.
- ☐ Say a thank-you prayer to God.

My Faith Choice

This week I will try hard to show my love for God and others. I will

_____

- -

_____

_____

- -

_____

Pray, "Thank you, Holy Spirit, for helping me listen to God's Word. Amen."

Chapter Review

Draw a line to match the words on the left with their meanings.

WORDS

1. Last Supper

2. Mass

3. Eucharist

MEANINGS

The celebration in which we listen to the Word of God. We say thank you to God.

The sacrament in which we receive the Body and Blood of Christ.

The meal Jesus ate with his disciples on the night before he died.

Thank You, God

We can pray quietly in our hearts, and we can pray aloud.

Leader Let us remember Jesus. Think about Jesus. *(Pause.)*

All **Thank you, God.**

Leader Think about what Jesus told us about God. *(Pause.)*

All **Thank you, God.**

Leader Think about people who share God's love with you. *(Pause.)*

All **Thank you, God. Amen.**

With My Family

This Week . . .

In chapter 15, "We Go to Mass," your child learned:

▶ The Mass is the most important celebration of the Church.

▶ During the Liturgy of the Word, we listen to the readings from the Bible.

▶ In the Liturgy of the Eucharist, we remember and do what Jesus did at the Last Supper. The bread and wine become the Body and Blood of Jesus.

▶ We receive the Body and Blood of Christ in Holy Communion.

For more about related teachings of the Church, see the *Catechism of the Catholic Church*, 1322–1405, and the *United States Catholic Catechism for Adults*, pages 215–227.

◼ Sharing God's Word

Read together Matthew 26:26–29 the account of the Last Supper. Or read the adaptation of the story on page 139. Emphasize that at Mass the bread and wine become the Body and Blood of Christ. Discuss the importance of participating during Mass.

◼ We Live as Disciples

The Christian home and family is a school of discipleship. Choose one of the following activities to do as a family, or design a similar activity of your own.

▶ At the end of Mass we are dismissed with these or similar words, "Go in peace, glorifying the Lord by your life." Choose one thing your family can do together to love and serve the Lord this week.

▶ Your child has learned that perseverance means that we try our best even when it is hard. Discuss times that this might be hard to do and that the Holy Spirit will help them.

◼ Our Spiritual Journey

The Psalms are prayers that represent an array of faith experiences. They are both personal and communal. They heighten our memory of God's loving plan of Creation and Salvation. Pray them at times of joy and sadness, lament, and thanksgiving. Choose and memorize a variety of verses from the Psalms. Pause throughout the day to pray them.

For more ideas on ways your family can live as disciples of Jesus, visit **www.BeMyDisciples.com**

CHAPTER 16

Jesus Shows God's Love

? Which foods are your family's favorites?

Healthy foods help us to grow. Jesus shared food with many people. Listen to part of one of those stories.

At the Last Supper, Jesus said to his disciples, "When you eat this bread and drink this wine, remember me."

BASED ON LUKE 22:19–20

? How do these words from the Bible remind you of the Mass?

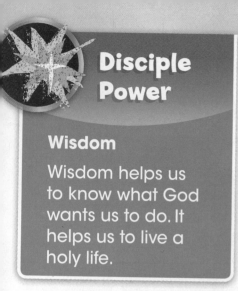

Disciple Power

Wisdom

Wisdom helps us to know what God wants us to do. It helps us to live a holy life.

CRS' Operation Rice Bowl

Read to Me

The Bible has many stories of Jesus sharing a meal with people. Like Jesus, we can share food with people too.

Each year during Lent, many Catholics participate in Operation Rice Bowl. Catholics put a small box on the table where they eat. Each family member puts money in the box.

At the end of Lent, Catholic families bring the box with the money to church. All the boxes are collected.

The Church uses the money to provide food and clean drinking water to people who need it. When we help people in need, we are sharing God's love too.

? What is one way that you can share God's love with people?

OPERATION RICE BOWL
Catholic Relief Services

www.orb.crs.org

Jesus Shares God's Love

Many of the first disciples of Jesus lived in **Galilee**. Galilee was the place where Jesus did much of his teaching. He also helped many people who lived there.

Some people in Galilee were fishermen. They fished in the Sea of Galilee for their food. Other people were farmers. They grew fruit and barley. They made bread from the barley.

Activity

Find the names on the map. Write the words in the right places in the sentences.

- Jesus was born in
  _____
  -
  _____.

- Jesus lived in
  _____
  -
  _____.

- Jesus ate fish from the Sea of
  _____
  -
  _____.

Find these places on the map. Circle the words on the map.

Nazareth

Sea of Galilee

Bethlehem

Saint Maria de Jesus

Sister Maria spent much of her life serving people who were poor and ill. Sister Maria loved going to Mass. Receiving Holy Communion helped her care for people as Jesus did. On May 21, 2000, Pope John Paul II named her Mexico's first woman saint.

Jesus Feeds the People

One time Jesus was teaching near the Sea of Galilee. A very large crowd of people gathered to hear Jesus. This is what happened.

It became late and the people were hungry. But Jesus' followers had only five loaves of bread and two fish. Jesus took the bread and the fish and prayed. His followers gave the food to the people. Everyone ate until they were full.

BASED ON MATTHEW 14:15–16, 19–20

Activity

Use the picture to tell a partner the story of Jesus feeding the people.

Jesus Cares for People

The story of Jesus sharing the bread and fish tells about a **miracle**. A miracle is something only God can do. It is a special sign of God's love.

The story of Jesus feeding the people shows how Jesus shared God's love with the people. Jesus took care of the people.

Jesus asks us to take care of one another too. This is one way we share God's love with people.

? How do you share God's love with other people?

Catholics Believe

Grace

The word *grace* means "gift." Grace is the gift of God's life and love. Grace helps us to share God's love with people. It helps us to live as children of God.

I Follow Jesus

The Holy Spirit helps you to show God's love and care for others. The Holy Spirit's gift of wisdom can help you to make good choices for living a holy life. When you share God's love, you are living a holy life.

Activity

Sharing God's Love

In the space write about or draw yourself sharing God's love with others.

My Faith choice

I will share God's love with my family. I will

_____

- -

_____.

Pray, "Thank you, Jesus, for teaching me how to share God's love. Amen."

Chapter Review

Read again the story of Jesus feeding the people. Number the sentences in the order they happen in the story.

_____ Everyone ate until they were full.

_____ Jesus took the five loaves and two fish and prayed.

_____ A large crowd was listening to Jesus. It was evening and they were hungry.

TO HELP YOU REMEMBER

1. Jesus saw that the people were hungry and gave them all enough to eat.

2. Jesus showed people that God cares for them.

3. Jesus teaches us to care for people.

A Blessing Prayer

Blessing prayers tell God we know that all good things come from him. Pray this blessing prayer together.

Leader Father, you care for everyone.

All **Blessed be God.**

Leader Jesus, you showed us how to care for people.

All **Blessed be God.**

Leader Holy Spirit, you help us to care for our families.

All **Blessed be God. Amen.**

With My Family

This Week . . .

In chapter 16, "Jesus Shows God's Love," your child learned:

► Jesus fed a large crowd with only five loaves of bread and two fishes (Matthew 14:15–20).

► This story tells that Jesus took care of people to remind them of God's love for them.

► This story is one of the miracle stories in the Gospels and reveals God's loving care for people and all creation.

► Wisdom is a gift of the Holy Spirit. It helps us to know God's will for us and to make good choices.

For more about related teachings of the Church, see the *Catechism of the Catholic Church*, 302–308 and 547–550, and the *United States Catholic Catechism for Adults*, pages 79–80, 215–216, and 222–223.

■ Sharing God's Word

Read together Matthew 14:15–20 the account of Jesus feeding the crowd. Or read the adaptation of the story on page 146. Emphasize that everyone ate until they were full. Discuss that this is a sign of God's caring love for all people.

■ We Live as Disciples

The Christian home and family is a school of discipleship. Choose one of the following activities to do as a family, or design a similar activity of your own.

► Jesus fed the hungry people to show them that God loves and cares for them. Choose to do one thing this week to show people that God loves and cares for them.

► When you go grocery shopping this week, purchase food to donate to the local food pantry. Join with others to be a sign of God's loving care for all people.

■ Our Spiritual Journey

A blessing prayer is an expression of God's generosity and love. Our life can be a blessing prayer. The best way to bless God is to share our material and spiritual blessings with others, especially people in need. Pray the blessing prayer on page 149 together as a family.

For more ideas on ways your family can live as disciples of Jesus, visit **www.BeMyDisciples.com**

Unit 4 Review

A. Choose the Best Word

Complete the sentences. Color the circle next to the best choice.

1. Every Sunday the people of the Church gather to celebrate _____.

○ Confirmation   ○ Mass

2. At the _____, Jesus said, "This is my body" and "This is my blood."

○ Last Supper   ○ First Easter

3. Prayer is listening and talking to _____.

○ our parents   ○ God

4. We need to ask for _____ when we have hurt someone.

○ forgiveness   ○ punishment

5. Jesus fed a crowd with two fish and _____ loaves of bread.

○ two   ○ five

B. Show What You Know

Circle the number next to your favorite prayer. Tell your class when you can pray it.

1. The Sign of the Cross   **4.** The Hail Mary

2. The Our Father   **5.** Grace Before Meals

3. The Glory Be Prayer

C. Connect with Scripture

What was your favorite story about Jesus in this unit? Draw something that happened in the story. Tell your class about it.

D. Be a Disciple

1. *What saint or holy person did you enjoy hearing about in this unit? Write the name here. Tell your class what this person did to follow Jesus.*

_____

- -

_____

- -

_____

2. *What can you do to be a good disciple of Jesus?*

_____

- -

_____

_____

- -

_____

The Way to Heaven

One day a young man asked Jesus, "What must I do to live forever with God in heaven?" he asked. Jesus said, "Keep God's commandments."

The young man said, "I have always kept them." "Wonderful!" Jesus said. "Now sell all your things, give to the poor, and follow me."

The young man turned away. He did not want to give away his things. Jesus felt sad. "If a person loves their things more than they love God, it will be hard to get to heaven."

BASED ON MARK 19:16–23

What I Have Learned

What is something you already know about these faith words?

Christians

_____

- -

_____

The Ten Commandments

_____

- -

_____

Faith Words to Know

Put an **X** next to the faith words you know.
Put a **?** next to the faith words you need
to learn more about.

Faith Words

____ The Great
Commandment

____ respect

____ community

____ worship

____ honor

A Question I Have

What question would you like to ask about
The Ten Commandments?

_____

- -

_____

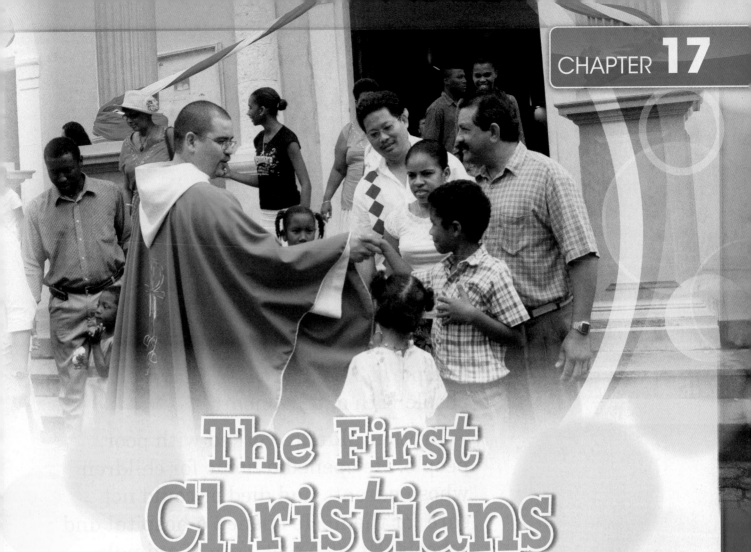

CHAPTER 17

The First Christians

? What are some things that make you and your family smile?

The first followers of Jesus were like a family. Listen to what the Bible tells us about Jesus' followers:

Jesus' followers were filled with joy and the Holy Spirit Based on Acts 13:52

? What do these words from the Bible tell you about Jesus' followers?

Understanding

God the Holy Spirit gives us the gift of understanding. Stories in the Bible help us understand God's love for us. Stories in the Bible help us understand what Jesus taught us.

The Church Follows **Jesus**

Saint Martin de Porres

Read to Me

Martin de Porres loved God. The Holy Spirit helped Brother Martin to live as a disciple of Jesus. Brother Martin served people with a joyful heart.

Brother Martin worked with poor people. He opened a home for children whose parents had died or could not care for them. He opened a hospital and schools. He also took care of animals that were sick or hungry.

The Church named Brother Martin a saint. Today many people follow the good example of Saint Martin de Porres.

? Who is someone you know who helps people as Saint Martin de Porres did?

Christians Share Stories

The Church tells stories that help us understand God's love for us. The Church tells stories about Jesus. These stories help us to know what it means to be a Christian. **Christians** are followers of Jesus Christ.

Our Church also shares stories about what Christians did a long time ago. We can read many stories about the first Christians in the New Testament.

Faith Focus
How did the people of the Church live when the Church began?

Faith Word
Christians
Christians are followers of Jesus Christ. They believe in Jesus Christ and live as he taught.

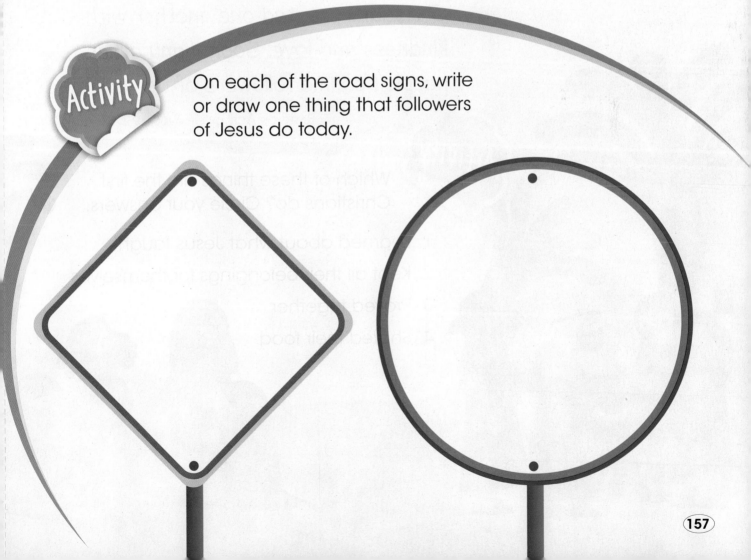

Activity

On each of the road signs, write or draw one thing that followers of Jesus do today.

Saint Paul the Apostle

Saint Paul became an apostle after Jesus' Resurrection. Paul traveled by land and by sea to teach people about Jesus. He invited them to believe in Jesus. The Church celebrates the feast day of Saint Paul the Apostle on June 29.

Christians Love One Another

This is a story about how the first Christians lived. It is a story that the Church has shared from her very beginning.

The first Christians spent time learning what Jesus taught. They shared their money and belongings with one another. They prayed together. They broke and shared bread together. Together they praised God.

Many people saw how the first Christians treated one another with kindness and love. Soon many other people became followers of Jesus.

BASED ON ACTS OF THE APOSTLES 2:42, 45–47

Activity

Which of these things did the first Christians do? Circle your answers.

1. Learned about what Jesus taught
2. Kept all their belongings for themselves
3. Prayed together
4. Shared their food

We Live as Jesus Taught

The first Christians did what Jesus did. They did what Jesus taught. Jesus taught us to love God and to love one another.

The stories about the first Christians teach us how to live as children of God. The first Christians showed their love for God. They prayed and shared the Eucharist. They thanked God for everything.

The first Christians showed their love for one another. They shared what they had with each other. They helped people in need.

Activity

Think of a follower of Jesus that you know. Check one thing that this person does. Act it out for your class.

Person I Know

- ☐ Prays with others
- ☐ Cares for others
- ☐ Tells me about Jesus
- ☐ Shares with me

I Follow **Jesus**

Each day you can try your best to live as Jesus taught. The Holy Spirit helps you to understand how Jesus wants you to treat people. You can treat people with kindness. This brings people joy. It also fills your heart with joy.

Activity

Write a ✓ mark in the box next to each thing that you can do this week to live as Jesus taught.

- ☐ Say my prayers.
- ☐ Play fairly.
- ☐ Hurt someone.
- ☐ Speak unkind words.
- ☐ Learn about Jesus.
- ☐ Help at home.
- ☐ Share my toys.
- ☐ Pay attention at school.
- ☐ Obey my parents.
- ☐ Be a litter-bug.

My Faith Choice

This week I will do one of the Christian acts that I have checked. I will

_____

- -

_____

Pray, "Thank you, Holy Spirit, for helping me to act as Christians do."

Chapter Review

*Read each sentence. Circle **Yes** if the sentence is true. Circle **No** if it is not true.*

1. The first Christians shared stories about Jesus.

   Yes   No

2. The first Christians prayed together.

   Yes   No

3. The first Christians shared their belongings with one another.

   Yes   No

► **TO HELP YOU REMEMBER**

1. Christians believe in Jesus Christ and do what he taught.

2. The first Christians gathered together and loved God and one another.

3. Christians today show their love for one another just as the first Christians did.

Praise the Lord

A sign of peace shows that we want to live as Jesus taught. We share a sign of peace at Mass.

Leader   We thank you, God, for the Church.

All   **Praise the Lord, for he is good!**

Leader   Let us share a sign of peace with one another.

All   **(Share a handshake or other sign of peace and friendship.)**

With My Family

This Week . . .

In chapter 17, "The First Christians," your child learned:

▶ The first Christians gathered to express their faith and belief in Jesus.

▶ The first Christians listened to the teachings of the Apostles. They shared all that they had with one another, especially with people in need. They gathered to pray and share the Eucharist.

▶ Christians today do the same things that the first Christians did. Every member of the Church is called to cooperate with the grace of the Holy Spirit and work together to live as Jesus taught.

▶ The Holy Spirit helps us to understand ways to live as followers of Jesus.

For more about related teachings of the Church, see the *Catechism of the Catholic Church*, 849–852, 1397, and 2030–2046, and the *United States Catholic Catechism for Adults*, pages 118–119.

■ Sharing God's Word

Read together the Acts of the Apostles 2:42–47, an account of the life of the first Christians. Or read the adaptation of the story on page 158. Emphasize that the first Christians shared with people in need and were known for their love for one another.

■ We Live as Disciples

The Christian home and family is a school of discipleship. Choose one of the following activities to do as a family, or design a similar activity of your own.

▶ Identify ways that your family lives as the first Christians did. Talk about ways you pray, learn about Jesus, and share things as a family. Invite each family member to choose one thing that they can do to help your family live as a Christian family.

▶ Decide one way in which your family can share your time and possessions with other people in your parish or neighborhood. For example, write get well cards to those who are sick or homebound.

■ Our Spiritual Journey

The peace that comes from living in communion with God, others, and all of Creation is the ultimate destination of our spiritual journey. You have received the gift of understanding to help you begin to achieve that peace. Pray the prayer on page 161 at mealtime and include a sign of peace.

For more ideas on ways your family can live as disciples of Jesus, visit **www.BeMyDisciples.com**

CHAPTER 18

We Love God

? What are some good rules for a family?

God's rules are called commandments. Listen to what the Bible tells us about them:

> God said, "I will show love to those who love me and keep my commandments."

BASED ON EXODUS 20:6

? What is one of God's rules that you know?

Knowledge

The gift of knowledge helps you to know and to follow God's rules. It also helps you to know things that are against God's rules and not to do them.

The Church Follows **Jesus**

Building Churches Read to Me

God has given us ten important rules called the Ten Commandments. Catholics follow the Ten Commandments. The First Commandment tells us to keep God first in our lives. Here is a story of how Father Richard followed the First Commandment.

Father Richard studied art before he became a priest. He also worked as an engineer. After he became a priest, Father Richard used his gifts to live the First Commandment. He helped build new churches and repair old churches.

Catholics gather in churches to worship God. Our churches show that we love God above all else.

❓ How do the people of your church help you to keep God first in your life?

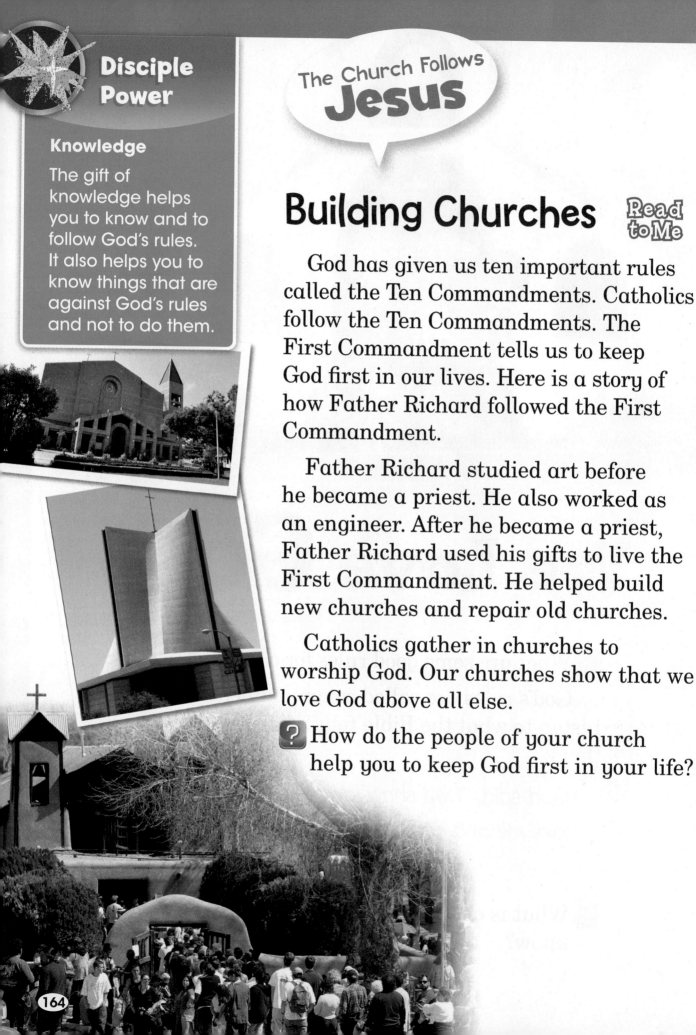

God's Commandments

We have rules at home, at school, and in our community. Good rules help us to live together in peace.

The Bible tells us that God gave us ten very special rules. These rules are the **Ten Commandments**. He gave us the Ten Commandments because he loves us. The Ten Commandments are the laws that God has given us to live as children of God.

The Ten Commandments tell us how we are to love God and other people. They tell us to care for ourselves and for all creation.

Faith Focus
Why did God give us the Ten Commandments?

Faith Words
Ten Commandments
The Ten Commandments are the ten laws that God has given us to help us live as children of God.

worship
We worship God when we love and honor God more than anyone and anything else.

Activity

With your classmates, act out one way you can show your love for God. Act out one way you can show your love for your family.

Jesus Teaches Us

Jesus taught us that we are to live the Ten Commandments. Jesus showed us how to love God. Jesus prayed to his Father. He always did what God the Father asked him to do.

Jesus showed us how to love one another. He was kind to everyone. Jesus told us to treat people as he did. He said,

"I give you this new commandment. You are to love one another as I have loved you."

BASED ON JOHN 13:34

? How are the people in the pictures showing their love for God? How are they showing their love for people?

We Love God

The First, Second, and Third Commandments tell us ways to show our love for God.

The First Commandment tells us that we are to **worship** only God. We are to love God more than anything and anyone else.

The Second Commandment tells us to honor God. We are to speak God's name with love and respect.

The Third Commandment tells us to keep Sunday as a holy day. Every Sunday, we gather with our Church family for Mass. We give thanks and praise to God for all that he has done for us.

Activity

Thank God for all that he has done for you. Use words and pictures to make a Thank You card.

Thank You, God, for...

I Follow Jesus

You are learning about the Ten Commandments. Your family and the Church will help you. The Holy Spirit will always help you to know the Ten Commandments and to live them. The Holy Spirit's gift of knowledge helps you to worship and honor God.

Activity

A Letter to God

Write a letter. Tell God how you will show your love for him this week.

Dear God,

_____

- -

_____

_____

- -

_____.

My Faith Choice

Read the letter you wrote to God. Write one way you will show your love for God this week.

_____

- -

_____

Pray, "Thank you, Holy Spirit, for helping me to show my love for you."

Chapter Review

Draw lines to match the words in column A with their meanings in column B.

Column A

1. First Commandment

2. Second Commandment

3. Third Commandment

Column B

a. Keep Sunday holy.

b. Worship only God.

c. Speak God's name with respect.

An Act of Love

When we pray an act of love, we tell God that we love him with all our hearts. Pray these words at home with your family. Pray them now with your class:

**O my God, you created me.
You share your love with me.
You are all good.
I love you with my whole heart.
Amen.**

With My Family

This Week . . .

In chapter 18, "We Love God," your child learned:

▶ God gave us the Ten Commandments.

▶ The Ten Commandments tell us ways to live as children of God.

▶ The First, Second, and Third Commandments tell us to love, honor, and worship God above all else.

▶ Jesus taught us to live the Ten Commandments. We are to love God and people as Jesus taught.

▶ Knowledge is one of the seven Gifts of the Holy Spirit. It helps us to know how we are to live and to follow God's will.

For more about related teachings of the Church, see the *Catechism of the Catholic Church*, 2052–2074, and the *United States Catholic Catechism for Adults*, pages 341–369.

■ Sharing God's Word

Read John 13:34–35 together, about Jesus giving his disciples the New Commandment, or you can read an adaptation of the story on page 166. Emphasize that Jesus by his example showed us how to love God and one another. He showed us how to live the Ten Commandments.

■ We Live as Disciples

The Christian home and family is a school of discipleship. Choose one of the following activities to do as a family, or design a similar activity of your own.

▶ Attend Mass together as a family on Sundays. Plan an activity for after Mass that the family can enjoy together.

▶ When you gather for dinner this week, invite family members to share one thing that they did that day to show their love for God.

■ Our Spiritual Journey

Knowing your way as you journey though life is vital. Knowing where you want to go and how to get there is essential. We can never reach our ultimate goal alone. Pray the prayer on page 169 with your family to help keep your priorities in life in the right order.

For more ideas on ways your family can live as disciples of Jesus, visit **www.BeMyDisciples.com**

CHAPTER 19

We Love Others

[?] What are some of the ways that you show your love for your family?

Listen to what the Bible tells us about God's Commandments:

God gave us the commandments so that we may live as friends with him and other people. BASED ON DEUTERONOMY 6:20–25

[?] What do the Commandments help us to do?

The Church Follows **Jesus**

Temperance

Having more things does not make us happy. Temperance helps us to know the difference between what we need and what we just want to have. It is important to know what will really make us happy.

Helping People in Need

Read to Me

Our parish helps us live as friends with God and one another. They help us to live the Ten Commandments.

Some parishes have a group called the Saint Vincent de Paul Society. This group helps people in need. Families give them things they do not really need. The group gives these things to people who do need them.

The group also helps people to visit doctors and dentists. They run camps in the summertime for children. The Saint Vincent de Paul Society shows people how much God loves them.

? What are some of the ways that you see people being kind to one another?

We Respect People

The rest of the Ten Commandments tell us that we are to **respect** other people and ourselves. We show respect when we treat and **honor** other people and ourselves as children of God. Showing respect is a way to show love.

We show respect to people in many ways. We listen carefully to one another. We are polite and kind. We are fair to one another.

We show respect to ourselves in many ways. We take care of our bodies. We act safely.

Faith Words

▶ **respect**
We show people respect when we love them because they are children of God.

▶ **honor**
We honor people when we treat them with great respect.

Activity With a partner, act out one way you can show respect to each other.

Faith-Filled People

Vincent de Paul

Saint Vincent de Paul showed us how to live the Ten Commandments. He treated all people with respect. He cared for people who were lonely. The Church celebrates the feast day of Saint Vincent de Paul on September 27.

We Care for Things

The Ten Commandments tell us to respect what belongs to us. It teaches us that we are to respect what belongs to other people, too. We are to take good care of the things that we have.

We show respect for what belongs to others. We are to ask before we borrow their things. We are to return the things that we borrow. We do not steal.

The Ten Commandments also teach us that we are to share our things with others.

? What is one way that you can care and share with others?

We Tell the Truth

The Ten Commandments teach us that we are to be honest. We are honest when we tell the truth. We are not being honest when we lie.

It is important to tell the truth. When we tell the truth, we show respect for ourselves and other people. Lying shows that we do not respect ourselves and other people. When we tell the truth, people trust us.

Activity

Look at the pictures. What could the children say to be honest?

_____

- -

_____

I Follow Jesus

When you are kind and fair, you treat people with respect. You love people as Jesus taught. When you tell the truth, you are a disciple of Jesus.

Activity

Fill in the blanks in the story.

I ask a friend, "May I please borrow your markers?

_____

- -

I will take good _____

of them." When I am finished, I will return the markers

"_____ "

- -

and say, _____.

My Faith Choice

Check (√) ways you will show respect for other people. I will

☐ tell the truth.   ☐ share my things.

☐ say kind words.   ☐ play safely.

 Pray, "Thank you, God, for teaching me to show respect for other people. Amen."

Chapter Review

*Read each sentence. Circle **Yes** if the sentence is true. Circle **No** if it is not true.*

1. Respecting others is a way to show love.

   Yes   No

2. Listening to one another shows respect.

   Yes   No

3. Taking care of what belongs to others shows respect.

   Yes   No

4. Telling lies shows respect.

   Yes   No

TO HELP YOU REMEMBER

1. We are to treat ourselves and others as children of God.

2. We are to show respect for other people.

3. We are to tell the truth.

Lord, Hear Our Prayer

Pray together:

Leader God, you love us. For people who are hungry, we pray,

All **Lord, hear our prayer.**

Leader For people who are sick, we pray,

All **Lord, hear our prayer.**

Leader Everyone pray quietly for someone. *(Pause.)*

All **Lord, hear our prayer.**

With My Family

This Week . . .

In chapter 19, "We Love Others," your child learned:

▶ The Fourth through Tenth Commandments tell us to love and respect other people, ourselves, and all God's creation.

▶ The last seven of the Ten Commandments name the ways that we are to live the second part of the Great Commandment and truly live as children of God.

▶ Temperance is a virtue that helps us to know the difference between what we need and what we simply want to have.

For more about related teachings of the Church, see the *Catechism of the Catholic Church*, 2052–2074, and the *United States Catholic Catechism for Adults*, pages 375–455.

■ Sharing God's Word

Read together Acts of the Apostles 2:42–47. Emphasize that this story tells about the first Christians living the Commandments as Jesus taught. Name the things that the first Christians did to show how they lived the Ten Commandments.

■ We Live as Disciples

The Christian home and family is a school of discipleship. Choose one of the following activities to do as a family, or design a similar activity of your own.

▶ Read together a children's book about treating people with respect. Discuss why showing respect is at the heart of our love for others.

▶ Have each family member create two lists of their possessions. In one list, write things that you really need. In the second list, write things you like but do not truly need. Choose items you might give away to a charitable group.

■ Our Spiritual Journey

We are a pilgrim people. We make our earthly journey together. In this chapter, your child prayed for others. This is called a prayer of intercession. Intercessory prayer is a prayer that we offer on the behalf of others. Read and pray together the prayer on page 177.

For more ideas on ways your family can live as disciples of Jesus, visit **www.BeMyDisciples.com**

CHAPTER 20

We Live as a Community

? Who do you know in your neighborhood?

Jesus taught us how to live together.

Jesus said, "Love God with all your heart, with all your soul, and with all your mind. This is the first and greatest commandment. The second is like this one: Love others as much as you love yourself." BASED ON MATTHEW 22:34–39

? How do good neighbors and friends treat each other?

Disciple Power

Justice

We practice justice when we treat people fairly. People who are just live as Jesus taught.

The Church Follows **Jesus**

Saint Peter Claver

Peter Claver did what Jesus taught. He helped people who were being treated unjustly. They had been taken from their homes in Africa. They were being sold as slaves.

The guards tried to stop Peter from going on the ships, but he would not be stopped. God gave him strength. Peter was a very brave man.

The ship was hot and dirty. The people had no water to drink or to wash with. Many of them were very sick. Peter Claver cared for them. Many became followers of Jesus.

? How did Saint Peter Claver follow Jesus?

God's Family

A **community** is a group of people who respect and care for one another. People in a community help one another.

We all belong to the community of God's people. God makes each of us special. God blesses each of us with gifts and talents. We respect each other's gifts. God asks us to use our gifts to live as a community.

Faith Focus
What does it mean to live the Great Commandment?

Faith Words
community
A community is a group of people who respect and care for one another.

Great Commandment
The Great Commandment is to love God above all else and to love others as we love ourselves.

Activity

How are the children in the pictures sharing their gifts? Tell a partner.

Good Rules Help Us

Good rules help us to live together in a community. They help us to respect one another. The rules that a community makes are called laws.

Good laws help a community to live together in peace. Good laws help people to have the things that they need to live. Good laws help us to live God's laws.

God's laws help us to know right and wrong. They help us to make good choices. They help us to respect one another and to care for one another. God's laws help us to live as children of God.

Activity

Follow the road in the picture. Circle a favorite place. Tell one way that you can live as a child of God there.

The Great Commandment

God wants all people to love him with their whole hearts. He wants all people to love and respect others as they love themselves. We call this the **Great Commandment**. It is also called the Great Law of God.

The Great Commandment helps us to live as the community of God's people. Jesus showed us how to live the Great Commandment.

Jesus gave us the gift of the Church. The Church helps us to live the Great Commandment.

Circle **G** next to ways that you can show love for God. Circle **P** next to ways that you can show love for yourself and other people.

Living the Great Commandment

G	P	Pray.
G	P	Say kind words.
G	P	Act fairly.
G	P	Take part in Mass.
G	P	Forgive others.

I Follow Jesus

The Holy Spirit helps you to live the Great Commandment. He helps you to love God above all else. He helps you to treat others with justice and with respect.

Activity

Living God's Laws

Finish each sentence. Write what you can do to live as a good member of your family, school, or parish.

_____

1. I can share my _____.

_____

2. I can help by _____.

_____

3. I can pray for _____.

My Faith Choice

Look at what you wrote in the activity. Which one will you do this week? I will

_____

_____

Pray, "Thank you, Jesus, for teaching me the Great Commandment. Thank you, Holy Spirit, for helping me to live the Great Commandment. Amen."

Chapter Review

Find and circle the three words hidden in the puzzle. Share with a partner what each word tells about the Great Commandment.

GOD	LOVE	PEOPLE

```
L  H  L  O  V  E  T  Y
Q  L  P  G  O  D  M  U
P  E  O  P  L  E  B  D
```

TO HELP YOU REMEMBER

1. The Great Commandment teaches us that we are to love God and to love other people as we love ourselves.

2. The Great Commandment helps us to follow Jesus.

3. The Great Commandment helps us to live as good members of our community.

Teach Me, Lord

The Bible has many prayers. This prayer is part of a psalm. Learn the words of this prayer by heart. Pray them each day. Ask God to help you live the Great Commandment.

Lord God, teach me your ways.
You are my God and Savior.

BASED ON PSALM 25:4–5

With My Family

This Week . . .

In chapter 20, "We Live as a Community," your child learned:

▶ Communities make laws to help people live together in peace. Good laws help us to live God's laws. God gives us laws to help us show our love for God, for ourselves, and for other people.

▶ The Great Commandment is the summary of all God's laws. The Church helps us to live God's Law and the good laws that communities make.

▶ The virtue of justice helps us to treat everyone fairly. When we treat people fairly, we live the Great Commandment.

For more about related teachings of the Church, see the *Catechism of the Catholic Church*, 1877–1942, 1949–1974, and 2234–2246, and the *United States Catholic Catechism for Adults*, pages 307–309.

◼ Sharing God's Word

Read Matthew 22: 34-40 about Jesus teaching the Great Commandment. Emphasize that the Great Commandment has two parts. We are to love God, and we are to love all people as we love ourselves.

◼ We Live as Disciples

The Christian home and family is a school of discipleship. It is the first place where children should learn to live as disciples of Jesus. Choose one of the following activities to do as a family or design a similar activity of your own.

▶ Good rules help us to live together. Talk about your family's good rules and how they help you to live together.

▶ Choose an activity to do this week to live the Great Commandment.

◼ Our Spiritual Journey

The Ten Commandments are written on the heart of each person. They guide us toward living as God created us to live. They are the pulse of living the righteous life described in the Bible—that is, of our living in "right order" with God, with other people, and with all of creation. This week, pray as a family the psalm verse on page 185.

For more ideas on ways your family can live as disciples of Jesus, visit **www.BeMyDisciples.com**

Unit 5 Review

Name _____

A. Choose the Best Word

Complete the sentences. Color the circle next to the best choice.

1. The Great _____ is to love God with our whole heart and to love others as we love ourselves.

⭘ Commandment ⭘ Prayer

2. We show people _____ when we treat them as children of God.

⭘ respect ⭘ fear

3. The first _____ gathered together and showed how much they loved God and one another.

⭘ family ⭘ Christians

4. The Great Commandment helps us to live as good members of our _____.

⭘ community ⭘ team

5. The Ten Commandments teach us to _____ God.

⭘ respect ⭘ disobey

B. Show What You Know

Match the two columns. Draw a line from the words in column A to their meanings in column B.

Column A

1. community

2. worship

3. honor

Column B

a. Give praise and honor to God

b. To treat people with great respect

c. People who care for one another

C. Connect with Scripture

What was your favorite story about Jesus in this unit? Draw something that happened in the story. Tell your class about it.

D. Be a Disciple

1. *What saint or holy person did you enjoy hearing about in this unit? Write the name here. Tell your class what this person did to follow Jesus.*

_____

- -

_____

_____

- -

_____

2. *What can you do to be a good disciple of Jesus?*

_____

- -

_____

_____

- -

_____

The Good Shepherd

Shepherds take care of sheep. A good shepherd knows each sheep by name. The sheep come when they hear the shepherd's voice.

One day Jesus said to his friends, "I am the Good Shepherd. I know you all by name. I care for you. I love you so much I will give up my life for you. You are mine. You belong to me."

BASED ON JOHN 10:2–14

What I Have Learned

What is something you already know about these faith words?

Heaven

_____

- -

_____

parables

_____

- -

_____

Faith Words to Know

Put an **X** next to the faith words you know.
Put a **?** next to the faith words you need to learn more about.

Faith Words

____ Kingdom of God ____ glory ____ sin

____ joy ____ charity ____ peace

A Question I Have

What question would you like to ask about saints?

_____

- -

_____

CHAPTER 21

Jesus and the Children

? How do people show that they are friends?

Jesus invites everyone to be his friends. Listen to what the Bible tells us:

> Jesus said, "I call you my friends. I taught you everything that I learned from God, my Father."   BASED ON JOHN 15:15

? How do we know that Jesus wants us to be his friends?

The Church Follows **Jesus**

Joy

We live with joy when we recognize that happiness does not come from money or possessions. True happiness comes from knowing and following Jesus.

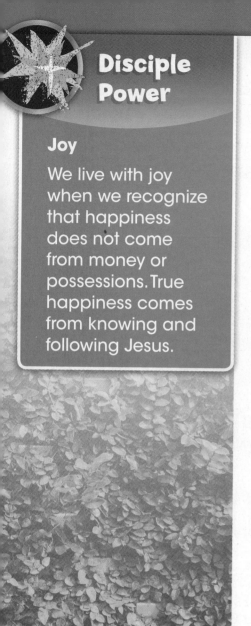

Children Helping Children

One cold day, a ten-year-old boy from France named Charles was out walking. He came upon another boy who was selling roasted chestnuts. Charles noticed that the boy was not wearing shoes. Charles took off his own shoes and gave them to the boy.

Charles grew up and became a priest and then a bishop. In 1839, Bishop Charles traveled from France to the United States and saw many poor children. Later, he asked children in France to help poor children in the United States. This was the beginning of the Holy Childhood Association.

Today children all over the world pray and help children in need.

? What are some ways that you can help other children?

The Holy Childhood Association's Sister Merieti Riiki with children.

Children of God

Faith Focus
Why are all children so special to Jesus?

Jesus showed that every person is special. He showed that God loves everyone. Jesus treated everyone as a child of God.

Jesus cured people who were sick. He was kind to people whom others did not like. Jesus forgave people who sinned. He loved those who wanted to hurt him.

Faith Word
Kingdom of God
The Kingdom of God is Heaven. Heaven is happiness with God forever.

Activity

Look at the pictures of Jesus. With a partner, talk about what Jesus is doing or saying. How is he treating people as children of God?

"Love your enemies and do good to them."

Saint Nicholas

Saint Nicholas tried to help children without being noticed. Many children leave their shoes out on December 6, the day that we celebrate the feast of Saint Nicholas. They hope that Saint Nicholas will fill their shoes with treats.

Jesus Welcomes Children

Here is a story from the Bible. It tells about Jesus inviting children to come to him.

People brought their children to Jesus.
But the disciples told them to go away.
Jesus said,
"Let the children come to me."
Then he blessed the children.

BASED ON MARK 10:13–14,16

Jesus invites all people to come to him. All people are invited to live in the **Kingdom of God**. The Kingdom of God is Heaven. Heaven is happiness with God forever.

Activity

Draw yourself in the picture. Ask Jesus to bless you.

We Are Children of God

In the Bible story, Jesus taught that all children are special to God. Some children have big, bright eyes. Others have a happy smile. Some are very quiet. Others talk all the time. All children are very different. Our differences show how special we are.

We treat all people as children of God. We do our best to live as children of God. We trust and love God with our whole heart.

❓ Why are all the children in the pictures special to God? Tell a partner.

I Follow Jesus

Jesus loves all children. Jesus loves you. The Holy Spirit helps you to share Jesus' love for others. True happiness comes from living as a child of God.

Activity

Use words and pictures to make an "I Care" button.

I Care

My Faith Choice

Underline one way that you will treat others as children of God. This week I will

1. invite a classmate to play with me.
2. tell my family I love them.
3. help out at home.

Pray, "Thank you, Jesus, for teaching me to treat others as children of God."

Chapter Review

Use one of these words to fill in the missing word in each sentence.

everyone	Heaven	invites

_____

- - - - - - - - - - - - - - - - - - - -

1. God loves _____.

_____

- - - - - - - - - - - - - - - - - - - -

2. The Kingdom of God is _____.

_____

- - - - - - - - - - - - - - - - - - - -

3. Jesus _____ everyone to follow him.

Let the Children Come

Our imaginations can help us talk to Jesus and listen to him.

1. Sit quietly in a comfortable position.

2. Imagine that you are going with your family to see Jesus.

3. Imagine that you are talking and listening to Jesus.

4. Spend a minute quietly listening to what Jesus might be saying to you.

With My Family

This Week . . .

In chapter 21, "Jesus and the Children," your child learned:

▶ God loves all people and wants them to live with him forever in Heaven.

▶ Children of God share God's love with one another.

▶ We live with joy when we recognize that happiness does not come from money or possessions. True happiness comes from knowing and following Jesus.

For more about related teachings of the Church, see the *Catechism of the Catholic Church*, 541–550 and 2816–2821; and the *United States Catholic Catechism for Adults*, pages 67, 68, and 310.

■ Sharing God's Word

Read together the Bible story in Mark 10:13–16 about Jesus blessing the children, or you can read the adaptation of the story on page 194. Emphasize that Jesus invited the children to come to him and blessed them.

■ We Live as Disciples

The Christian home and family is a school of discipleship. Choose one of the following activities to do as a family, or design a similar activity of your own.

▶ Jesus welcomed everyone. He showed people that God loves them. As a family, do one thing that will show people that God loves them.

▶ Discuss the ways in which your parish welcomes children. Name activities, events, and opportunities that are available for children in your parish. Make an effort to participate in one of them.

■ Our Spiritual Journey

Your child prayed a prayer of meditation in this chapter. This kind of prayer is also sometimes called *guided imagery*. Talk with your child about how our imaginations can help us to pray and to be with Jesus. It can help us talk and listen to Jesus. Provide a time and space for quiet prayer in your family. Visit a church together outside of Mass time and spend a few moments in quiet meditation.

For more ideas on how your family can live as disciples of Jesus, visit **www.BeMyDisciples.com**

CHAPTER 22

We Are Children of God

❓ What are some ways that people are different from one another?

All people are unique. No two people are exactly alike. People have different personalities, and special talents. We have different skin, hair, and eye colors. We even speak different languages. The Bible, however, tells us that all people are the same in one important way.

God created people in his image.

BASED ON GENESIS 1:27

❓ How are all people the same?

Disciple Power

Gentleness

Gentle people act calmly. They avoid actions that might lead others to anger or feeling hurt. They treat all people as children of God.

The Church Follows **Jesus**

The Sisters of the Blessed Sacrament

Read to Me

Katharine Drexel cared for all people. She treated everyone as a child of God.

Saint Katharine began the Sisters of the Blessed Sacrament. They work with African Americans and Native Americans. They work in schools and colleges. They work in cities and on the lands where Native Americans live.

The Sisters of the Blessed Sacrament treat all people as children of God. They teach others to treat all people with respect, fairness, and gentleness.

❓ What are some of the ways that you see people treating one another as children of God?

Children of God

God created all people out of love. God created people in his image and likeness. God created all people to know, love, and serve him.

All people are part of God's family. We are part of God's family. We are **children of God**. Children of God love God and love one another. Our kind words and actions show others that we love them and care about them.

Faith Focus
What does it mean to be a child of God?

Faith Words
children of God
All people are children of God. God created all people in his image.

glory
Glory is another word for praise.

Activity

Work with a partner to show what the word gentle means. Act it out without any words.

Faith-Filled People

Saint Josephine Bakhita

Josephine Bakhita was a young African girl. She was kidnapped and forced into the slave trade in Africa. When she was in her teens, she was left with the Canossian Sisters in Venice, Italy. There she came to know about God. Bakhita became a sister. She comforted the poor and encouraged others. Her feast day is February 8.

God Gives Us the Gift of Life

God is our loving Father. God shares the gift of his life with us. We are children of God. Children of God take very good care of the gift of life.

We respect and take care of the gift of our own lives. We respect and take care of the lives of other people.

? How do you take care of the gift of your own life?

We Show Our Love for God

God created us to know and to love him. Jesus taught about God's love. He showed people God's love with his actions. He spoke to people about God's love. Jesus taught that God wants us to be happy with him now and forever in Heaven.

Jesus showed us how to love God. We show our love for God when we help other people. We show our love for God when we pray. When we take care of creation, we are showing our love for God.

We give **glory** to God when we do these things. Children of God are to give glory to God in all they do and say.

Activity

Write a sentence that tells about one way you show your love for God.

_____

- -

_____

- -

_____

I Follow Jesus

God created you and all people to be children of God. The Holy Spirit helps you to treat all people as children of God.

Activity

Being Gentle

Draw yourself acting in a gentle way. Share your work with a partner.

My Faith Choice

Check (√) how you will live as a child of God.
This week I will

☐ be kind.

☐ pray.

☐ help my family.

☐ care for God's creation.

 Pray, "Thank you, Holy Spirit, for helping me to treat all people as children of God."

Chapter Review

Use this number code. Find out the important message about ourselves.

A	C	D	E	G	H	I	L	N	O	R	S	W
1	2	3	4	5	6	7	8	9	10	11	12	13

$\underline{\hphantom{xx}}$ $\underline{\hphantom{xx}}$ $\underline{\hphantom{xx}}$ $\underline{\hphantom{xx}}$ $\underline{\hphantom{xx}}$
13   4   1   11   4

$\underline{\hphantom{xx}}$ $\underline{\hphantom{xx}}$ $\underline{\hphantom{xx}}$ $\underline{\hphantom{xx}}$ $\underline{\hphantom{xx}}$ $\underline{\hphantom{xx}}$ $\underline{\hphantom{xx}}$
1   8   8   5   10   3   12

$\underline{\hphantom{xx}}$ $\underline{\hphantom{xx}}$ $\underline{\hphantom{xx}}$ $\underline{\hphantom{xx}}$ $\underline{\hphantom{xx}}$ $\underline{\hphantom{xx}}$ $\underline{\hphantom{xx}}$ $\underline{\hphantom{xx}}$
3   6   7   8   3   11   4   9

► TO HELP YOU REMEMBER

1. God created all people in his image.

2. God gives us the gift of life.

3. We are to take care of the gift of life.

The Glory Prayer

All Christian prayer gives glory to God. Learn the Glory Be Prayer by heart. Pray it each day in English or Spanish.

**Glory be to the Father
and to the Son
and to the Holy Spirit,
as it was in the beginning
is now, and ever shall be
world without end. Amen.**

Here is the prayer in Spanish.

**Gloria al Padre, al Hijo y al Espíritu Santo.
Como era en el principio, ahora y siempre,
por los siglos de los siglos. Amén.**

With My Family

This Week . . .

In chapter 22, "We Are Children of God," your child learned:

▶ God created all people in his image and likeness. God created all people out of his infinite love.

▶ God calls all people to be responsible stewards of the gift of life. We are called to show our love for God, especially in the way that we treat other people.

▶ We are to care for and treat our own lives and the lives of all people with gentleness.

For more about related teachings of the Church, see the *Catechism of the Catholic Church*, 355–361 and 1699–1709; and the *United States Catholic Catechism for Adults*, pages 67–68.

◾ Sharing God's Word

Read together 1 John 3:1. Emphasize that in Baptism we are joined to Jesus and become adopted children of God. We are to live as Jesus taught.

◾ We Live as Disciples

The Christian home and family is a school of discipleship. Choose one of the following activities to do as a family, or design a similar activity of your own.

▶ All people have the dignity of being children of God. Children of God are to love God and one another. Talk together about how your family can live as children of God. What kinds of words and actions show others that we love and care about them?

▶ Look through a children's magazine or picture book with your child. Point out all the pictures that show people living as children of God.

◾ Our Spiritual Journey

Giving glory and praise to God is so important that we are reminded to glorify God as we are sent forth at the end of Mass. In the Concluding Rites, the priest blesses us in the name of the Father, and of the Son, and of the Holy Spirit. We are then sent forth to do good works, praising and blessing the Lord with these words, "Go in peace, glorifying the Lord by your life." As a family, choose one thing you can do this week to glorify the Lord. Also, help your child to memorize the Glory Be Prayer on page 205 and pray it daily together.

For more ideas on ways your family can live as disciples of Jesus, visit **www.BeMyDisciples.com**

CHAPTER 23

Jesus Teaches about Love

? Which stories can you think of that help you make good choices?

Jesus sometimes told stories to teach us how to live as his disciples.

Jesus asked, "Who was the good neighbor in the story?" Someone replied, "The traveler who helped the man lying on the road." Jesus said, "You are right. Now, you treat other people the same way." BASED ON LUKE 10:36–37

? What do these words from the Bible tell you about Jesus?

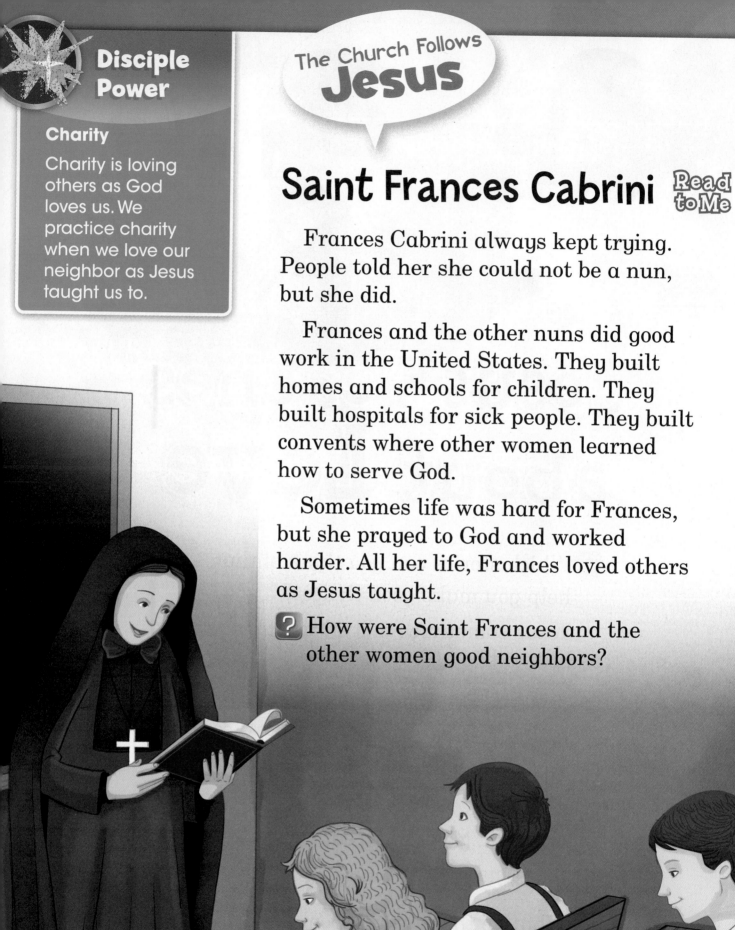

Disciple Power

Charity

Charity is loving others as God loves us. We practice charity when we love our neighbor as Jesus taught us to.

Saint Frances Cabrini Read to Me

Frances Cabrini always kept trying. People told her she could not be a nun, but she did.

Frances and the other nuns did good work in the United States. They built homes and schools for children. They built hospitals for sick people. They built convents where other women learned how to serve God.

Sometimes life was hard for Frances, but she prayed to God and worked harder. All her life, Frances loved others as Jesus taught.

❓ How were Saint Frances and the other women good neighbors?

Jesus Teaches Love

Jesus' disciples called him "Teacher." In Jesus' times, this was a great honor and a sign of respect. As other teachers did, Jesus often used stories to teach.

One kind of story Jesus told is called a **parable**. In a parable, the teacher compares two things. The teacher uses one thing that his listeners know well to help them understand the main point of the story.

The parables that Jesus told helped his listeners to know and love God better. These parables also tell us how much God loves us. These parables show us how to live as good neighbors and children of God.

Faith Word
parable
A parable is a story that compares two things. Jesus told parables to help people to know and love God better.

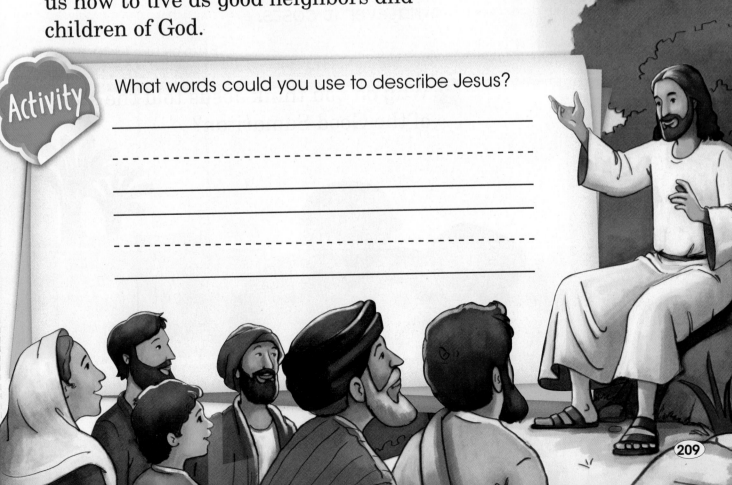

Activity

What words could you use to describe Jesus?

_____

- - - - - - - - - - - - - - - - - - -

_____

- - - - - - - - - - - - - - - - - - -

_____

Faith-Filled People

Saint Isidore the Farmer

Isidore spent much of his life working on a farm in Spain. He and his wife, also a saint, showed their love for God by being kind to their neighbors. Although they were poor, Isidore and Maria shared their food with those poorer than they were. Isidore is the patron saint of farmers and migrant workers. The Church celebrates his feast day on May 15.

The Good Samaritan

The stories that Jesus told are in the Gospels. The Gospels are in the New Testament. Here is one story that Jesus told. He said,

One day robbers attacked a man on a road. They hurt the man and left him lying on the road.

A traveler from Samaria saw the injured man. He stopped and put bandages on the man's wounds. The Samaritan brought the injured man to an inn. He told the innkeeper, "Take care of this man. I will pay you whatever it costs."

BASED ON LUKE 10:30, 33–35

? Why do you think Jesus told the story of the Good Samaritan?

A Good Neighbor

The story of the Good Samaritan helps us to live as followers of Jesus. It teaches that God wants us to help one another. God wants us to help people even when we do not feel like helping. This story teaches us to be good neighbors to one another.

Prayer of the Faithful

We are good neighbors when we pray for one another. Each Sunday at Mass, we pray the Prayer of the Faithful. In this prayer we pray for the Church, people who are sick, and people who have died.

Finish the picture story. Draw or write about how the children can act as good Samaritans.

1.

2.

3.

I Follow Jesus

You can be a good neighbor. You can show people how much God loves them and cares about them.

Activity

Living as a Good Neighbor

Color a ☺ next to two ways that you can help someone this week as Jesus taught, and then write one other way that you can help.

☺ Say kind words to someone who is sad.

☺ Help to fold laundry at home.

☺ Give a get-well card to someone.

☺ _____

My Faith Choice

I will do one of the things in the activity above. I will

_____

 Pray, "Thank you, Jesus, for teaching me to be a good neighbor."

Chapter Review

*Read each sentence. Circle **Yes** if the sentence is true. Circle **No** if it is not true.*

1. Jesus told stories called parables.

    Yes   No

2. The Good Samaritan took care of the injured man.

    Yes   No

3. Jesus told stories to teach us to help others.

    Yes   No

TO HELP YOU REMEMBER

1. Jesus told the parable of the Good Samaritan to help us to live as his followers.

2. God wants us to care for others.

3. We show charity when we love our neighbors.

We Pray for Others

We pray the Prayer of the Faithful at Mass. We pray for other people.

Leader   Dear God, help us show love. For the pope and Church leaders,

All   **Lord, hear our prayer.**

Leader   For our country's leaders,

All   **Lord, hear our prayer.**

Leader   Think of the people you wish to pray for. *(Pause.)*

All   **Lord, hear our prayer.**

With My Family

This Week ...

In chapter 23, "Jesus Teaches about Love," your child learned:

▶ Parables in the Bible help us come to know, love, and serve God.

▶ The parable of the Good Samaritan teaches us how we are to live as disciples of Jesus.

▶ We are to care about one another and to show our love by our actions as Jesus did.

▶ We practice charity when we love our neighbor as Jesus has taught us.

For more about related teachings of the Church, see the *Catechism of the Catholic Church*, 546; and the *United States Catholic Catechism for Adults*, pages 27–31, 79–80.

■ Sharing God's Word

Read together the parable of the Good Samaritan in Luke 10:29–37, or you can read the adaptation of the parable on page 210. Emphasize that the Samaritan was a good neighbor because he stopped and took the time to help the injured man.

■ We Live as Disciples

The Christian home and family is a school of discipleship. Choose one of the following activities to do as a family, or design a similar activity of your own.

▶ This week when you take part in the celebration of Mass, help your child pray the Prayer of the Faithful. After Mass, talk about the petitions that were used in the prayer.

▶ Talk about how your family can be good neighbors and show charity to one another this week. For example, help one another out without having to be asked.

■ Our Spiritual Journey

A prayer of the faithful is a prayer of intercession. Intercessory prayer is one of the Church's five main forms of prayer. In this chapter, your child prayed a prayer of the faithful. As the community of the faithful, we pray the Prayer of the Faithful at Mass or during the Liturgy of the Hours. Because these are the prayer intentions of the community, not individual people, appropriate subjects for the prayer have a communal nature. Subjects may include the Church and her ministers, civil leaders, the world and its people, those who are sick or dying, those who have died, those who are grieving, and anyone celebrating a sacrament. Read and pray together the prayer on page 213.

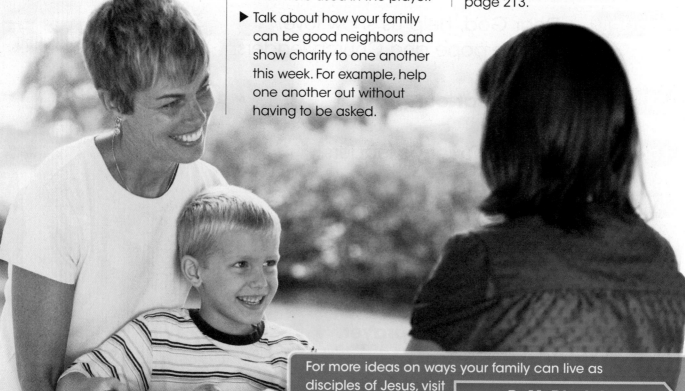

For more ideas on ways your family can live as disciples of Jesus, visit **www.BeMyDisciples.com**

CHAPTER 24

The Our Father

❓ Who has helped you to learn something new?

Many people help us to learn new things. Jesus taught his disciples how to pray.

Jesus said, "Pray to God privately. God will see you and reward you. Speak from your heart and God will hear you. God knows what you need."

BASED ON MATTHEW 6:6–8

❓ What do these words from the Bible tell you about prayer?

Disciple Power

Humility
Humility helps us know that all good things come from God.

The Church Follows **Jesus**

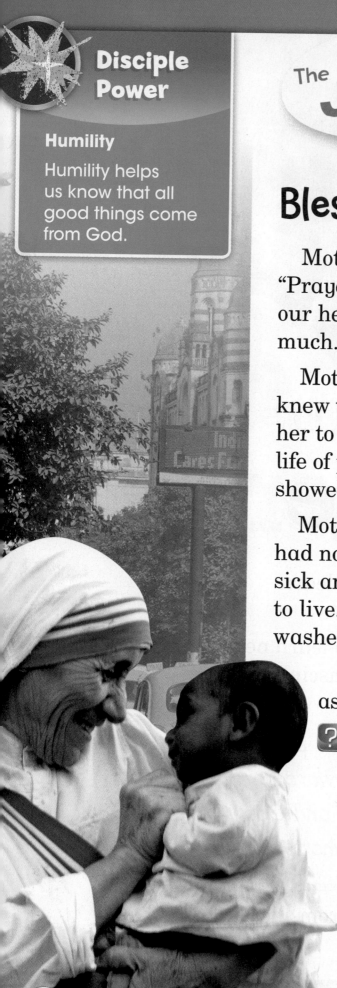

Blessed Teresa

Read to Me

Mother Teresa of Calcutta once said, "Prayer brings our heart closer to God. If our heart is close to God we can do very much."

Mother Teresa was very humble. She knew that praying often every day helped her to care for other people. Through a life of prayer and caring for others, she showed that God is everyone's Father.

Mother Teresa took care of people who had no one else. These people were very sick and very poor. They had no place to live. Mother Teresa fed them. She washed them.

The Church honors Mother Teresa as Blessed Teresa of Calcutta.

❓ What can you do to show that God is everyone's Father?

Jesus Prayed

Jesus prayed often. He talked to God his Father about everything. He listened to God the Father. He always did what his Father wanted him to do.

The followers of Jesus were with Jesus when he prayed. They saw him pray. They wanted to learn to pray as he prayed.

Faith Focus
What prayer did Jesus teach us to pray?

Faith Word
Our Father
The Our Father is the prayer Jesus taught his disciples.

Activity

In each picture frame draw a picture of someone who has helped you to pray. Write the person's name under the picture.

Faith-Filled People

Sister Thea Bowman

Sister Thea had the gift of singing. Singing was one way Sister Thea prayed. Everywhere she went, Sister Thea sang about God's love for everyone. She praised God in everything she did. She lived the words of the Our Father every day.

The Our Father

One day one of the disciples asked Jesus to teach them to pray. Jesus said,

"This is how you are to pray.
Our Father in heaven,
 hallowed be your name,
 your kingdom come,
 your will be done,
  on earth as in heaven.
 Give us today our daily bread;
 and forgive us our debts, as we
 forgive our debtors;
and lead us not into temptation,
but deliver us from evil."

BASED ON MATTHEW 6:9–13

These words of the **Our Father** teach us how to live as disciples of Jesus. They are a summary of the entire Gospel.

Activity

In the space, draw one thing you need that you want to ask God to give you.

Jesus Teaches Us to Pray

When we pray the Our Father, we tell God that we believe he is our Father. We honor the name of God. We trust him with all our hearts.

We ask God the Father to help us to live as his children. We ask for forgiveness. We tell God that we forgive those who hurt us. We ask him to help us to do what is good. We pray that we will live with him forever in Heaven.

Catholics Believe

The Lord's Prayer

The Lord's Prayer is another name for the Our Father. This is because Jesus our Lord gave us this prayer.

Activity

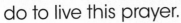

The Lord's Prayer

The children in the picture are bringing the Lord's Prayer to life. In the space draw what you could do to live this prayer.

I Follow Jesus

When you pray the Our Father, you show that you trust God. You show that everything good comes from God. You show that you believe that everyone is a child of God.

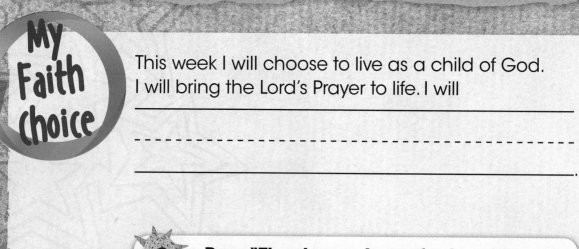

Activity

Check (√) where you can pray the Our Father.

☐ At Mass

☐ At Home

☐ On the school bus

☐ In the car

☐ In the park

My Faith Choice

This week I will choose to live as a child of God. I will bring the Lord's Prayer to life. I will

_____

- -

_____.

 Pray, "Thank you, Jesus, for teaching me to pray the Our Father."

Chapter Review

Find and circle the words in the puzzle. Use each word in a sentence. Tell a partner.

Jesus	forgive	Father	prayer

```
F O R G I V E T P
M C J E S U S W Z
O P R A Y E R K H
L P R F A T H E R
```

TO HELP YOU REMEMBER

1. Jesus taught us to pray the Our Father.

2. The Our Father is a prayer for all God's children.

3. The Our Father is also called the Lord's Prayer.

The Our Father

Every day Christians all around the world pray the Our Father.

Leader Let us pray the Our Father together. Our Father, who art in heaven, hallowed be thy name;

All **thy kingdom come; thy will be done on earth as it is in heaven.**

Leader Give us this day our daily bread; and forgive us our trespasses

All **as we forgive those who trespass against us; and lead us not into temptation, but deliver us from evil. Amen.**

With My Family

This Week . . .

In chapter 24, "The Our Father," your child learned that:

▶ Jesus gave the Our Father to his first disciples.

▶ Jesus gave this wonderful prayer to all Christians of all times.

▶ Praying the Our Father teaches us to pray. It is a summary of the entire message of the Gospel.

▶ Humility is a virtue that reminds us of our right place before God. It helps us know that all we have is a gift from God.

For more about related teachings of the Church, see the *Catechism of the Catholic Church*, 2759–2856; and the *United States Catholic Catechism for Adults*, pages 483–492.

■ Sharing God's Word

Read Matthew 6:9–13 together, the account of Jesus teaching the disciples to pray the Our Father. Or read the adaptation of the story on page 218. Emphasize that praying the Our Father honors God the Father and shows our trust in him.

■ We Live as Disciples

The Christian home and family is a school of discipleship. Choose one of the following activities to do as a family, or design a similar activity of your own.

▶ Practice saying the words of the Our Father with your child. When you take part in the celebration of Mass this week, help your child join in praying the Our Father.

▶ Use the Our Father as your mealtime prayer this week. Remember that the Our Father is the prayer of all God's children. Christians pray the Our Father every day all around the world.

■ Our Spiritual Journey

Saint Augustine called the Our Father the summary of the Gospel. Pray the Our Father as a prayer of meditation. Praying and living by the Our Father will create in you a pure and humble heart—a heart that keeps God and his love for you at the heart, or center, of your life. Make sure that your children know this prayer by heart.

For more ideas on how your family can live as disciples of Jesus, visit **www.BeMyDisciples.com**

Unit 6 Review

A. Choose the Best Word

Complete the sentences. Color the circle next to the best choice.

1. The Good Samaritan story teaches us that God wants us to _____ one another.

○ respect   ○ care for

2. God made all people _____.

○ in his image   ○ happy

3. God wants us to _____ Heaven.

○ live in   ○ remember

4. Mother Teresa was very _____.

○ proud   ○ humble

5. Jesus taught the disciples to pray the

_____.

○ Hail Mary   ○ Our Father

B. Show What You Know

Circle the numbers next to the words that tell about the Bible story of the Good Neighbor.

1. parable   **4.** an innkeeper

2. a man from Samaria   **5.** care for one another

3. a camel

C. Connect with Scripture

What was your favorite story about Jesus in this unit? Draw something that happened in the story. Tell your class about it.

D. Be a Disciple

1. *What saint or holy person did you enjoy hearing about in this unit? Write the name here. Tell your class what this person did to follow Jesus.*

_____

- -

_____

- -

_____

2. *What can you do to be a good disciple of Jesus?*

_____

- -

_____

- -

_____

We Celebrate the Church Year

The Year of Grace

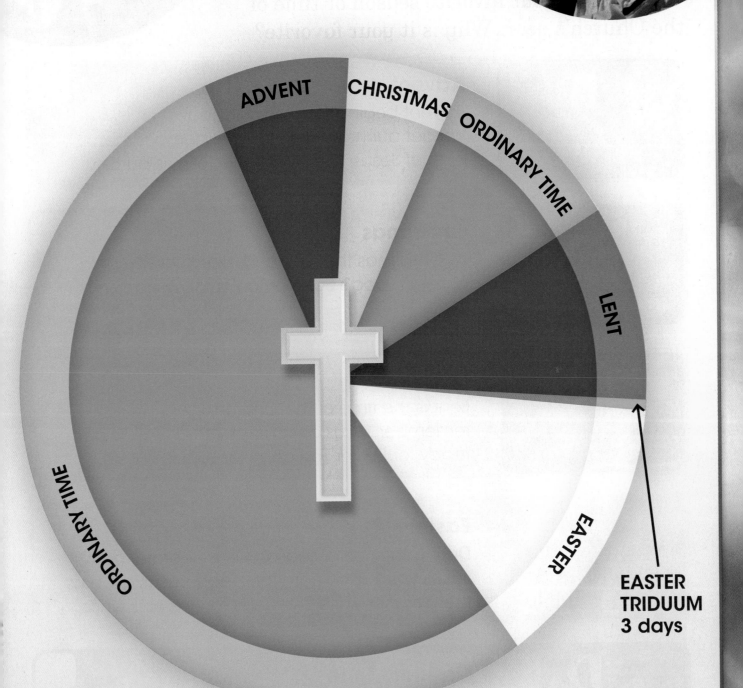

ADVENT

CHRISTMAS

ORDINARY TIME

LENT

EASTER

ORDINARY TIME

EASTER TRIDUUM
3 days

The Liturgical Year

The Church's year of prayer and worship is called the liturgical year.

Check (✓) your favorite season or time of the Church's year. Why is it your favorite?

Advent
Advent begins the Church's year. We get our hearts ready to remember the birth of Jesus. The color for Advent is purple.

Christmas
At Christmas the Church celebrates the birth of Jesus, God's Son. The color for Christmas is white.

Lent
Lent is the time of the Church's year we remember Jesus died for us. It is a time to get ready for Easter. The color for Lent is purple.

Easter
During the Easter season we celebrate that Jesus was raised from the dead. Jesus gave us the gift of new life. The color for Easter is white.

Ordinary Time
Ordinary Time is the longest time of the Church's year. The color for Ordinary Time is green.

Solemnity of All Saints

Saints are people who love God very much. They are holy people. They are members of our Church family who show us how to be good disciples of Jesus. Some saints are adults. Other saints are children. Saints come from all cultures and all nations. They live with Jesus in Heaven.

God wants each of us to become a saint. We pray to the saints to help us live as God's children. Mary, the mother of Jesus, is the greatest saint. We pray to Mary, too.

The saints hear our prayers and want us to be happy with God. The Church honors all saints on November 1 each year. This feast is the Solemnity of All Saints.

Mary, Saint Thérèse of Lisieux, Saint Andrew, and Saint Martin de Porres

The Greatest Saint

Draw a picture of Mary doing what God asks.
Also draw a picture of yourself helping Mary.

My Faith Choice

This week I will show my love for God by

_____

- -

_____.

Pray, "Mary, help me to love God and follow Jesus. Amen."

Advent

The Church's season of Advent begins the Church's year. During Advent we prepare for Christmas. We light candles to chase away the winter darkness. These candles remind us that Jesus is the Light of the world.

Jesus asks us to be lights for the world too. During Advent we let our light shine. We help people. We make gifts. We do secret good deeds for each other.

We gather in church and prepare our hearts to welcome Jesus. We sing and pray together. We remember that Jesus is with us every day.

My Light Shines

Decide what you can do to get ready for Christmas. Color in the flames to show what you can do.

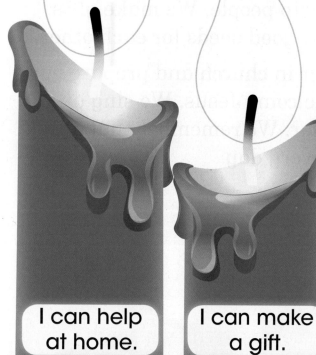

I can help
at home.

I can make
a gift.

I can help
a neighbor.

I can
pray.

My
Faith
choice

During Advent I will share the light of Jesus. I will

_____

- -

_____.

 Pray, "Jesus, you are the Light of the world! Amen."

The Immaculate Conception

Mary is a very special mother. God the Father chose Mary to be the mother of Jesus. Jesus is the son of Mary and the Son of God.

God blessed Mary more than any other person. The Bible tells us that God said to Mary

You are blessed among all women.

BASED ON LUKE 1:42

God did this because he chose Mary to be Jesus' mother.

God was with Mary in a special way all of her life. Mary was born without sin. Mary never sinned. This is what we mean when we pray, "Hail Mary, full of grace, the Lord is with thee."

We celebrate this special blessing God gave Mary each year. We celebrate the Immaculate Conception on December 8th. We honor Mary, and we honor God. We thank God for the special way that he blessed Mary.

Hail Mary

Tell Mary how special she is. Decorate the space around these words from the Hail Mary. Pray this first part of the prayer with your class.

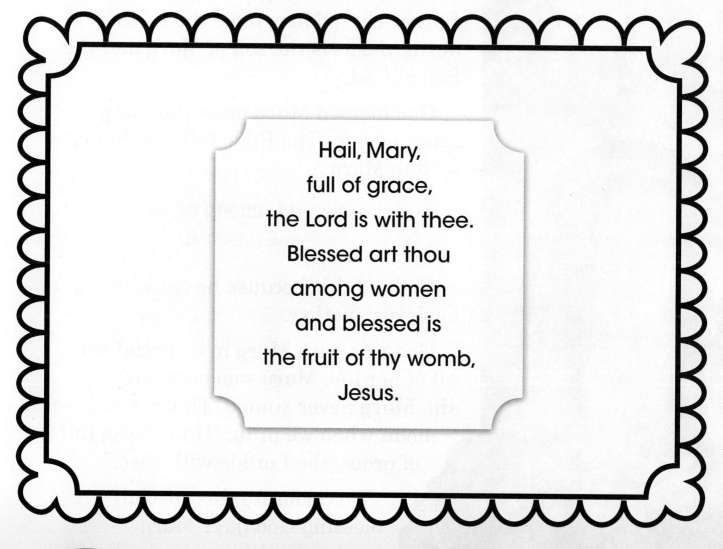

Hail, Mary,
full of grace,
the Lord is with thee.
Blessed art thou
among women
and blessed is
the fruit of thy womb,
Jesus.

My Faith Choice

This week I will honor Mary. I will learn to pray the Hail Mary by heart.

Pray, "Mary, God loves you. I love you too. Blessed are you! Amen."

Faith Focus
Who does our
Blessed Mother
Mary want us
to love?

Our Lady of Guadalupe

Our Blessed Mother Mary loves all people. One day Mary told a man named Juan Diego how much she loves us.

Juan Diego lived in Mexico. One day as he was walking to Mass, Juan saw a lady. This lady was Mary.

Mary gave Juan a message to give his bishop. She wanted the bishop to build a church in her name. Mary gave Juan roses to show the bishop. Juan rolled the roses up in his cloak and took them to the bishop. When he opened his cloak, everyone was very surprised at what they saw. There was a beautiful image of Mary on the cloth.

The Church that the bishop built is named Our Lady of Guadalupe. We celebrate the feast of Our Lady of Guadalupe on December 12.

Our Blessed Mother

Color the picture of Our Lady of Guadalupe. On the lines below the picture write, "I love you, Mary."

_____

- -

_____

My Faith Choice

This week I will honor Mary. I will try my best to love others. Draw a ☺ next to the actions that you will do.

_____ Be kind to a friend.

_____ Help at home.

_____ Return crayons that I borrow.

Pray, "Mary, Our Lady of Guadalupe. Help me to love God as you do. Amen."

Christmas

We like good news. It makes us happy. On the night of Jesus' birth, some shepherds heard good news. Angels said to them,

"Today in Bethlehem the savior God promised to send you has been born." BASED ON LUKE 2:11

The shepherds hurried to Bethlehem. They found Jesus there lying in a manger, just as the angels said. The shepherds were Jesus' first visitors. They told others all that happened.

We want to welcome Jesus just as the shepherds did. We thank God for bringing joy that will never end. We share the Good News with others.

Las Posadas

People in Mexico celebrate the journey of Mary and Joseph to the inn in Bethlehem. The words *las posadas* mean "the inns." You can perform this skit with your class.

Mary and Joseph   In the name of God, can we stay here?

Innkeeper One   We have no room for you. We are too crowded!

Mary and Joseph   In the name of God, do you have room for us?

Innkeeper Two   We have no room here.

Mary and Joseph   In the name of God, do you have room for us?

Innkeeper Three   My inn is full. There is a stable in the hills. It is warm there.

Reader   *Read Luke 2:1–20.*

Leader   God our Father, we rejoice in the birth of your Son. May we always welcome him when he comes. Amen.

My Faith Choice

This week I will treat others with love. I will

_____

- -

_____.

Pray, "May Jesus' birth bring joy, peace, and love to all people. Amen."

Mary, the Mother of God

Gifts make us feel special. When someone gives us a gift we know they care about us. God gave us the best gift. God the Father gave us Jesus, his Son. On Christmas day we celebrate the birth of Jesus.

God the Father chose the Blessed Virgin Mary to be the mother of his Son, Jesus. Mary is the Mother of God. The Blessed Virgin Mary is our mother, too. She loves and cares for all the children of the world.

We honor Mary, the Mother of God, in a special way on January 1. On this day we go to Mass. We give thanks to God for the gift of our Blessed Mother. What a special way to start the New Year!

A Mother's Love

Our Blessed Mother did many things for her Son, Jesus. She does them for us too. Find the words in the border. Tell your class about times that mothers do these things. Then decorate the border.

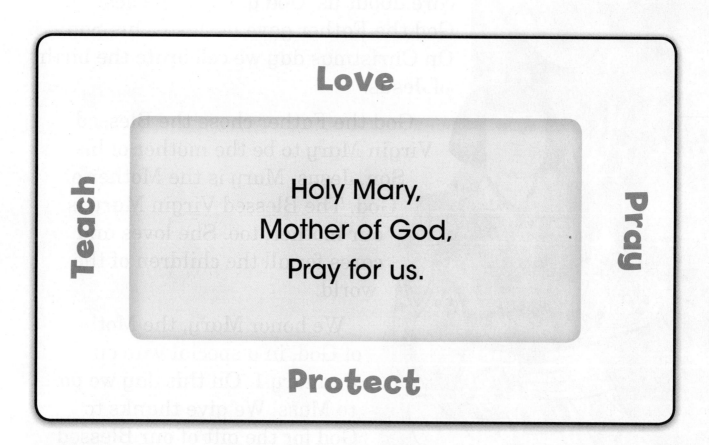

Love

Teach

Pray

Protect

Holy Mary,
Mother of God,
Pray for us.

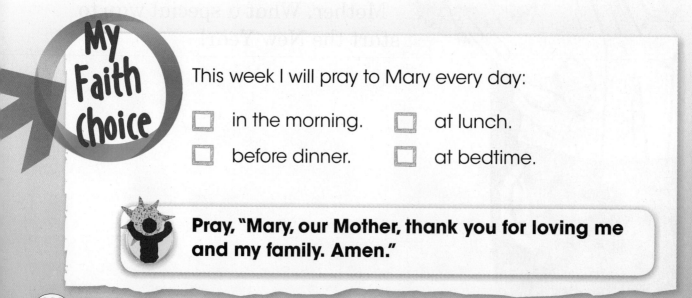

My Faith Choice

This week I will pray to Mary every day:

☐ in the morning.   ☐ at lunch.

☐ before dinner.   ☐ at bedtime.

Pray, "Mary, our Mother, thank you for loving me and my family. Amen."

Epiphany

During Advent we waited and prepared for Christmas. We waited and prepared to welcome Jesus, the Son of God.

On Epiphany we hear the story of the Magi. These wise men traveled a long distance to find Jesus. They went to Bethlehem and honored Jesus.

We want the whole world to celebrate the birth of the newborn Savior. We want Heaven and nature to sing and rejoice. Jesus is the Savior of the world.

We Announce the Birth of the Savior

Make the cover for a Christmas card. Draw a picture and use words. Tell everyone that Jesus is the Savior of the world.

The Magi honored Jesus. I will honor Jesus by

_____

- -

_____

 Pray, "Jesus, you are the Savior of the world! Amen."

Ash Wednesday

Prepare! That's what we do whenever something important is going to happen. Parents prepare for a new baby. They visit the doctor and get everything ready at home. Students prepare for tests so they can learn as much as possible.

The most important time of the year for the Church is Easter. Lent is the time when we prepare for Easter. Ash Wednesday is the first day of Lent. It is the first day of our preparation for Easter.

On Ash Wednesday we go to church. The sign of the cross is made on our foreheads with ashes. We pray and ask God to help us to be more like Jesus. We ask God to help us celebrate Lent.

Being Like Jesus

Lent is a special time of prayer. In the spaces put words or pictures to complete your prayer.

Dear God,

I praise and thank you for

.

I ask you to watch over

.

Keep them in your care.

Amen.

This week I will remember to pray as Jesus did. I will

_____

_____

.

 Pray, "Father in Heaven, thank you for helping me become more like your Son, Jesus. Amen."

Lent

Think about Spring. Remember how plants push their way up through the earth. Trees sprout leaves and buds. Birds sing their best songs.

During Spring we plant new seeds. We cut away dead twigs and stems. We prepare for new life.

Jesus talked about death and new life. He held up a seed and said,

"I say to you, unless a grain of wheat falls to the ground and dies, it remains just a grain of wheat; but if it dies, it produces much fruit."

John 12:24

During Lent we clear a place to plant seeds of faith and love. We work and pray. We grow in faith and love. We are getting ready for Easter.

New Life

Put this picture story in order. Number the pictures from 1 to 6. Share the story with a friend. Tell how the story helps us to understand Lent.

My Faith Choice

During Lent I can do good deeds and make sacrifices to get ready for Easter. I will

_____

- -

_____ .

Pray, "Thank you, Jesus, for helping us to change and grow during Lent. Amen."

Palm Sunday of the Lord's Passion

Sometimes important people come to our town or school. We go out and greet them. We cheer and rejoice!

Once Jesus came to the city of Jerusalem. He loved the people there. He wanted to gather them as a mother hen gathers her little chicks.

When Jesus came to the city, the people cheered. They waved branches from palm trees. They also spread their cloaks on the road to honor Jesus.

We remember this day at the beginning of Holy Week on Palm Sunday of the Lord's Passion. On this day we carry palm branches and honor Jesus too.

Honoring Jesus

These words are hidden in the puzzle. Find and circle the words. Use the words to tell a partner about Palm Sunday.

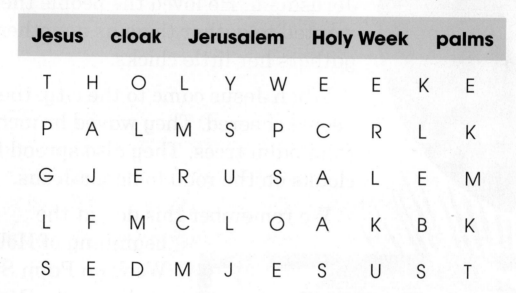

| Jesus | cloak | Jerusalem | Holy Week | palms |

```
T H O L Y W E E K E
P A L M S P C R L K
G J E R U S A L E M
L F M C L O A K B K
S E D M J E S U S T
```

My Faith Choice

On Palm Sunday, the beginning of Holy Week, I can honor Jesus. I will

_____

- -

_____.

Pray, "Hosanna in the highest! We rejoice and honor you, Jesus. Amen."

Holy Thursday

Holy Thursday is one of the most important days for our Church. On this day we remember and celebrate the day on which Jesus gave us the Eucharist.

On the night before he died, Jesus celebrated a special meal with his disciples. We call this meal the Last Supper. At the Last Supper Jesus took bread and said to the disciples, "This is my body." He also took a cup of wine and said, "This is the cup of my blood." Then Jesus said to them, "Do this in memory of me" (based on Luke 22:14–19).

We celebrate the Eucharist every time we celebrate Mass. When we do, we are doing what Jesus asked.

Thank You, Jesus!

Use the code to color the stained-glass window. Use the stained-glass window to tell what happened at the Last Supper.

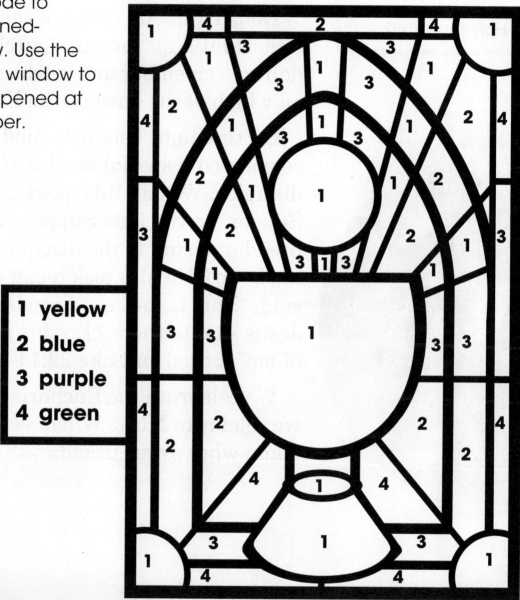

1 **yellow**
2 **blue**
3 **purple**
4 **green**

Jesus celebrated a special meal with his disciples and asked us to do the same. In Jesus' memory, I will

_____

- -

_____.

  Pray, "Thank you, Jesus, for your gift of the Eucharist. Amen."

Good Friday

Sometimes we look at pictures or a gift that someone has given us. This helps us to remember and think about that person. What do you look at to help you remember someone?

The Friday of Holy Week is called Good Friday. It is a very special day for all Christians. It is the day we remember in a special way that Jesus suffered and died for us.

On Good Friday the deacon or priest holds up a cross for us to look at. Looking at the cross, we think about and remember how much Jesus loves us. One way we show our love for Jesus is by loving one another.

Showing Our Love for Others

Draw a † next to the ways you can show your love for others. Write one more thing you will do.

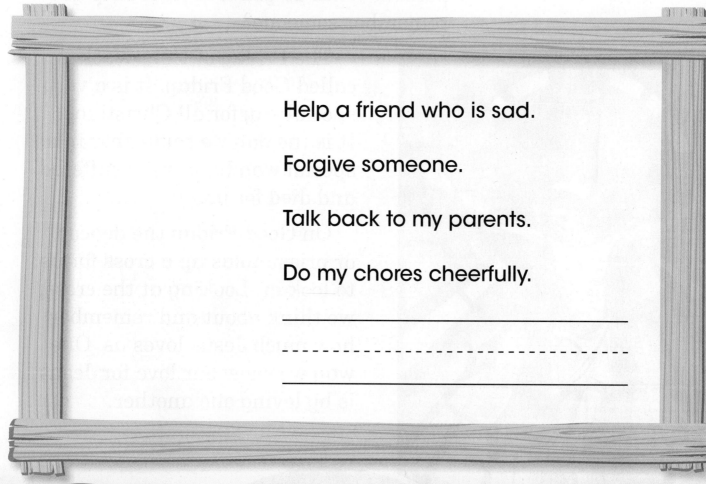

Help a friend who is sad.

Forgive someone.

Talk back to my parents.

Do my chores cheerfully.

_____

- -

_____

My Faith Choice

I will show that I am thankful that Jesus died out of love for us. I will

_____

- -

_____.

Pray, "We adore you and thank you, Jesus, for suffering and dying on the cross for us. Amen."

Easter Sunday

At Easter we see signs of new life all around us. These signs remind us that Jesus was raised from the dead to new life. We call this the Resurrection of Jesus. On Easter Sunday Christians celebrate Jesus' Resurrection.

We are Easter people! Alleluia is our song! We sing Alleluia over and over during the fifty days of the Easter season. The word *Alleluia* means "Praise the Lord!" We praise God for raising Jesus from the dead to new life.

Every Sunday in the year is a little Easter. We sing. We rest. We enjoy one another. All year long we praise and thank God.

Praise the Lord

Decorate the Easter banner. Use colors and words about new life. Show your finished banner to your friends and your family. Tell them about the Resurrection of Jesus.

This week I will give praise to the Lord. I will

_____

- -

_____

 Pray, "Jesus, you are risen. Alleluia!"

The Ascension

Forty days after Easter, Jesus led his disciples outside Jerusalem. He reminded them that he had suffered, died, and was raised to new life. Jesus said that we should share this good news with everyone.

Then he blessed the disciples and returned to his Father in Heaven. The Church celebrates the day Jesus returned to his Father. We call this day the Solemnity of the Ascension of the Lord.

Sing to Heaven

Sing this song. Use the melody to "Frère Jacques." Teach the song to your family and sing it together.

He is risen. He is risen.
Yes, he is. Yes, he is.
He will come in glory.
He will come in glory.
Yes, he will. Yes, he will.

Sound the trumpet.
Sound the trumpet.
He ascends. He ascends.
We await the Spirit.
We await the Spirit.
Yes, we do. Yes, we do.

Holy Spirit, Holy Spirit.
Come to us; come to us.
He will come and guide us.
He will come and guide us.
Yes, he will. Yes, he will.

Jesus asks us to share his good news with others. I will

_____

- -

_____.

Pray, "Bless us always, Jesus, as we wait for you to come again in glory. Amen."

Faith Focus
When does
the Holy Spirit
help us to live
as followers of
Jesus?

Pentecost

Sometimes we receive a gift that we use to help others. We have received that kind of gift from Jesus.

After Jesus returned to his Father, the disciples received the gift of the Holy Spirit. The Spirit helped them to share the Good News about Jesus with others. He helped them to do good work in Jesus' name.

On Pentecost Sunday, we remember that the Holy Spirit came to the disciples. We too have received the gift of the Holy Spirit. The Holy Spirit helps us to do good. When we do good things in Jesus' name, we lead others to Jesus.

The Gift of the Holy Spirit

Work with a partner and follow this maze. At each place, stop to share the Good News about Jesus with each other.

My
Faith
choice

This week I will honor the Holy Spirit. I will do good.
I will

_____

- -

_____.

 Pray, "Come, Holy Spirit, and fill my heart with your love. Amen."

Catholic Prayers and Practices

Sign of the Cross

In the name of the Father,
and of the Son,
and of the Holy Spirit. Amen.

Our Father

Our Father, who art in heaven,
hallowed be thy name;
thy kingdom come,
thy will be done
on earth as it is in heaven.
Give us this day our daily bread,
and forgive us our trespasses,
as we forgive those who trespass
   against us;
and lead us not into temptation,
   but deliver us from evil.
Amen.

Glory Be (Doxology)

Glory be to the Father
and to the Son
and to the Holy Spirit,
as it was in the beginning
is now, and ever shall be
world without end. Amen.

The Hail Mary

Hail, Mary, full of grace,
the Lord is with thee.
Blessed art thou among women
and blessed is the fruit
   of thy womb, Jesus.
Holy Mary, Mother of God,
pray for us sinners,
now and at the hour of our death.
Amen.

Signum Crucis

In nómine Patris,
et Fílii,
et Spíritus Sancti. Amen.

Pater Noster

Pater noster, qui es in cælis:
sanctificétur nomen tuum;
advéniat regnum tuum;
fiat volúntas tua,
   sicut in cælo, et in terra.
Panem nostrum cotidiánum
   da nobis hódie;
et dimítte nobis débita nostra,
sicut et nos dimíttimus debitóribus
   nostris;
et ne nos indúcas in tentatiónem;
sed líbera nos a malo. Amen.

Gloria Patri

Glória Patri
et Fílio
et Spirítui Sancto.
Sicut erat in princípio,
et nunc et semper
et in sæcula sæculórum. Amen.

Ave, Maria

Ave, María, grátia plena,
Dóminus tecum.
Benedícta tu in muliéribus,
et benedíctus fructus ventris tui,
   Iesus.
Sancta María, Mater Dei,
ora pro nobis peccatóribus,
nunc et in hora mortis nostræ.
Amen.

Apostles' Creed

(from the Roman Missal)

I believe in God,
the Father almighty,
Creator of heaven and earth,
and in Jesus Christ, his only Son,
    our Lord,

*(At the words that follow, up to and
including the Virgin Mary, all bow.)*

who was conceived by the Holy Spirit,
born of the Virgin Mary,
suffered under Pontius Pilate,
was crucified, died and was buried;
he descended into hell;
on the third day he rose again from
    the dead;
he ascended into heaven,
and is seated at the right hand of
    God the Father almighty;
from there he will come to judge the
    living and the dead.
I believe in the Holy Spirit,
the holy catholic Church,
the communion of saints,
the forgiveness of sins,
the resurrection of the body,
and life everlasting. Amen.

Nicene Creed

(from the Roman Missal)

I believe in one God,
the Father almighty,
maker of heaven and earth,
of all things visible and invisible.

I believe in one Lord Jesus Christ,
the Only Begotten Son of God,
born of the Father before all ages.

God from God, Light from Light,
true God from true God,
begotten, not made, consubstantial
    with the Father;
through him all things were made.
For us men and for our salvation
he came down from heaven,

*(At the words that follow, up to and
including and became man, all bow.)*

and by the Holy Spirit was incarnate
    of the Virgin Mary,
and became man.

For our sake he was crucified under
    Pontius Pilate,
he suffered death and was buried,
and rose again on the third day
in accordance with the Scriptures.
He ascended into heaven
and is seated at the right hand of
    the Father.
He will come again in glory
to judge the living and the dead
and his kingdom will have no end.

I believe in the Holy Spirit, the Lord,
    the giver of life,
who proceeds from the Father and
    the Son,
who with the Father and the Son is
    adored and glorified,
who has spoken through the prophets.

I believe in one, holy, catholic and
    apostolic Church.
I confess one Baptism for the
    forgiveness of sins
and I look forward to the resurrection
    of the dead
and the life of the world to come. Amen.

Morning Prayer

Dear God,
as I begin this day,
keep me in your love and care.
Help me to live as your child today.
Bless me, my family, and my friends
    in all we do.
Keep us all close to you. Amen.

Grace Before Meals

Bless us, O Lord,
    and these thy gifts,
which we are about to receive
    from thy bounty,
    through Christ our Lord.
Amen.

Grace After Meals

We give thee thanks,
    for all thy benefits, almighty God,
who lives and reigns forever. Amen.

Evening Prayer

Dear God,
I thank you for today.
Keep me safe throughout the night.
Thank you for all the good I did today.
I am sorry for what I have chosen
    to do wrong.
Bless my family and friends. Amen.

A Vocation Prayer

God, I know you will call me
for special work in my life.
Help me follow Jesus each day
and be ready to answer your call.
Amen.

Act of Contrition

My God,
I am sorry for my sins
    with all my heart.
In choosing to do wrong
and failing to do good,
I have sinned against you,
whom I should love above all things.
I firmly intend, with your help,
to do penance,
to sin no more,
and to avoid whatever leads me
    to sin.
Our Savior Jesus Christ
suffered and died for us.
In his name, my God, have mercy.
Amen.

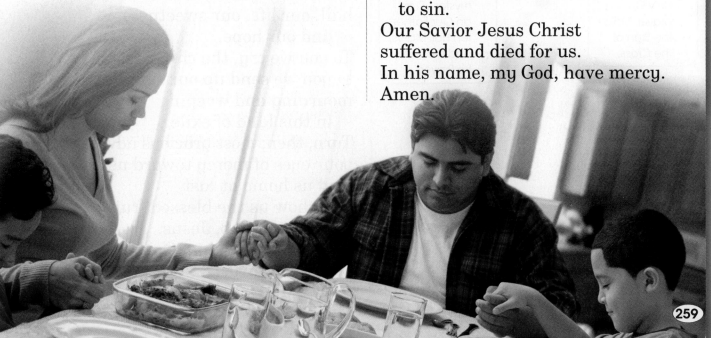

Rosary

Catholics pray the Rosary to honor Mary and remember the important events in the life of Jesus and Mary. There are twenty mysteries of the Rosary. Follow the steps from 1 to 5.

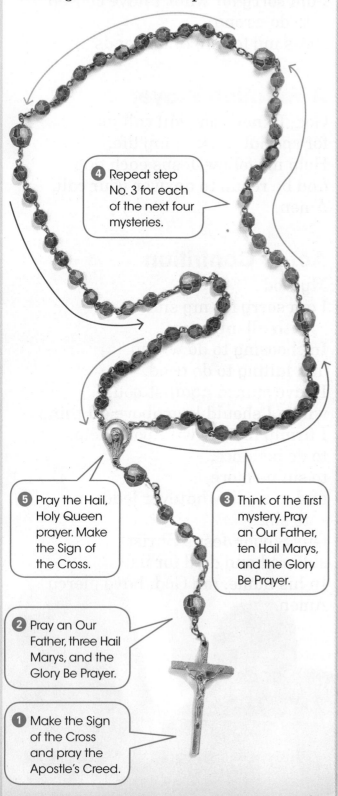

4 Repeat step No. 3 for each of the next four mysteries.

5 Pray the Hail, Holy Queen prayer. Make the Sign of the Cross.

3 Think of the first mystery. Pray an Our Father, ten Hail Marys, and the Glory Be Prayer.

2 Pray an Our Father, three Hail Marys, and the Glory Be Prayer.

1 Make the Sign of the Cross and pray the Apostle's Creed.

Joyful Mysteries
1. The Annunciation
2. The Visitation
3. The Nativity
4. The Presentation
5. The Finding of Jesus in the Temple

Mysteries of Light
1. The Baptism of Jesus in the Jordan River
2. The Miracle at the Wedding at Cana
3. The Proclamation of the Kingdom of God
4. The Transfiguration of Jesus
5. The Institution of the Eucharist

Sorrowful Mysteries
1. The Agony in the Garden
2. The Scourging at the Pillar
3. The Crowning with Thorns
4. The Carrying of the Cross
5. The Crucifixion

Glorious Mysteries
1. The Resurrection
2. The Ascension
3. The Coming of the Holy Spirit
4. The Assumption of Mary
5. The Coronation of Mary

Hail, Holy Queen

Hail, holy Queen, mother of mercy:
hail, our life, our sweetness,
　　and our hope.
To you we cry, the children of Eve;
to you we send up our sighs,
mourning and weeping
　　in this land of exile.
Turn, then, most gracious advocate,
your eyes of mercy toward us;
lead us home at last
and show us the blessed fruit
　　of your womb, Jesus.
O clement, O loving, O sweet
　　Virgin Mary.

The Ten Commandments

1. I am the LORD your God: you shall not have strange gods before me.
2. You shall not take the name of the LORD your God in vain.
3. Remember to keep holy the LORD's Day.
4. Honor your father and your mother.
5. You shall not kill.
6. You shall not commit adultery.
7. You shall not steal.
8. You shall not lie.
9. You shall not covet your neighbor's wife.
10. You shall not covet your neighbor's goods.

Based on Exodus 20:2–3, 7–17

Precepts of the Church

1. Participate in Mass on Sundays and holy days of obligation, and rest from unnecessary work.
2. Confess sins at least once a year.
3. Receive Holy Communion at least during the Easter season.
4. Observe the prescribed days of fasting and abstinence.
5. Provide for the material needs of the Church, according to one's abilities.

The Great Commandment

"You shall love the Lord, your God, with all your heart, with all your soul, and with all your mind. . . . You shall love your neighbor as yourself." Matthew 22:37, 39

The Law of Love

"This is my commandment: love one another as I love you." John 15:12

The Seven Sacraments

Jesus gave the Church the Seven Sacraments. The Seven Sacraments are signs of God's love for us. When we celebrate the Sacraments, Jesus is really present with us. We share in the life of the Holy Trinity.

Baptism

We are joined to Christ. We become members of the Body of Christ, the Church.

Confirmation

The Holy Spirit strengthens us to live as children of God.

Eucharist

We receive the Body and Blood of Jesus.

Reconciliation

We receive God's gift of forgiveness and peace.

Anointing of the Sick

We receive God's healing strength when we are sick or dying, or weak because of old age.

Holy Orders

A baptized man is ordained to serve the Church as a bishop, priest, or deacon.

Matrimony

A baptized man and a baptized woman make a lifelong promise to love and respect each other as husband and wife. They promise to accept the gift of children from God.

We Celebrate the Mass

The Introductory Rites

We remember that we are the community
of the Church. We prepare to listen to the Word of God
and to celebrate the Eucharist.

The Entrance

We stand as the priest, deacon, and other ministers enter the assembly. We sing a gathering song. The priest and deacon kiss the altar. The priest then goes to the chair, where he presides over the celebration.

Greeting of the Altar and of the People Gathered

The priest leads us in praying the Sign of the Cross. The priest greets us, and we say,

"And with your spirit."

The Penitential Act

We admit our wrongdoings.
We bless God for his mercy.

The Gloria

We praise God for all the good that he has done for us.

The Collect

The priest leads us in praying the Collect, or the opening prayer.
We respond, "Amen."

The Liturgy of the Word

God speaks to us today.
We listen and respond to God's Word.

The First Reading from Scripture

We sit and listen as the reader reads from the Old Testament or from the Acts of the Apostles. The reader concludes, "The Word of the Lord." We respond,

"Thanks be to God."

The Responsorial Psalm

The song leader leads us in singing a psalm.

The Second Reading from Scripture

The reader reads from the New Testament, but not from the four Gospels. The reader concludes, "The Word of the Lord." We respond,

"Thanks be to God."

The Acclamation

We stand to honor Christ, present with us in the Gospel. The song leader leads us in singing **"Alleluia, Alleluia, Alleluia,"** or another chant during Lent.

The Gospel

The deacon or priest proclaims, "A reading from the holy Gospel according to (name of Gospel writer)." We respond,

"Glory to you, O Lord."

He proclaims the Gospel. At the end he says, "The Gospel of the Lord." We respond,

**"Praise to you,
Lord Jesus Christ."**

The Homily

We sit. The priest or deacon preaches the homily. He helps the people gathered to understand the Word of God spoken to us in the readings.

The Profession of Faith

We stand and profess our faith. We pray the Nicene Creed together.

The Prayer of the Faithful

The priest leads us in praying for our Church and her leaders, for our country and its leaders, for ourselves and others, for those who are sick and those who have died. We can respond to each prayer in several ways. One way that we respond is,

"Lord, hear our prayer."

The Liturgy of the Eucharist

We join with Jesus and the Holy Spirit
to give thanks and praise to God the Father.

The Preparation of the Gifts

We sit as the altar table is prepared
and the collection is taken up.
We share our blessings with the
community of the Church and
especially with those in need. The
song leader may lead us in singing
a song. The gifts of bread and wine
are brought to the altar.

The priest lifts up the bread and
blesses God for all our gifts. He
prays, "Blessed are you, Lord God of
all creation . . ." We respond,

"Blessed be God for ever."

The priest lifts up the cup of wine
and prays, "Blessed are you, Lord
God of all creation . . . " We respond,

"Blessed be God for ever."

The priest invites us,
"Pray, brothers and sisters,
that my sacrifice and yours
may be acceptable to God,
the almighty Father."

We stand and respond,

**"May the Lord accept the
sacrifice at your hands for
the praise and glory of his
name, for our good, and the
good of all his holy Church."**

The Prayer over the Offerings

The priest leads us in praying the
Prayer over the Offerings.
We respond, **"Amen."**

266

Preface

The priest invites us to join in praying the Church's great prayer of praise and thanksgiving to God the Father.

Priest: "The Lord be with you."

Assembly: "And with your spirit."

Priest: "Lift up your hearts."

Assembly: "We lift them up to the Lord."

Priest: "Let us give thanks to the Lord our God."

Assembly: "It is right and just."

After the priest sings or prays aloud the preface, we join in acclaiming,

**"Holy, Holy, Holy Lord God of hosts.
Heaven and earth are full of your glory.
Hosanna in the highest.
Blessed is he who comes in the name of the Lord.
Hosanna in the highest."**

The Eucharistic Prayer

The priest leads the assembly in praying the Eucharistic Prayer. We call on the Holy Spirit to make our gifts of bread and wine holy and that they become the Body and Blood of Jesus. We recall what happened at the Last Supper. The bread and wine become the Body and Blood of the Lord. Jesus is truly and really present under the appearances of bread and wine.

The priest sings or says aloud, "The mystery of faith." We respond using this or another acclamation used by the Church,

"We proclaim your Death, O Lord, and profess your Resurrection until you come again."

The priest then prays for the Church. He prays for the living and the dead.

Doxology

The priest concludes the praying of the Eucharistic Prayer. He sings or prays aloud,

"Through him, and with him, and in him,
O God, almighty Father,
in the unity of the Holy Spirit, all glory and honor is yours,
for ever and ever."

We respond by singing, **"Amen."**

The Communion Rite

The Lord's Prayer
We pray the Lord's Prayer together.

The Sign of Peace
The priest invites us to share a sign of peace, saying, "The peace of the Lord be with you always." We respond,
  "And with your spirit."
We share a sign of peace.

The Fraction, or the Breaking of the Bread
The priest breaks the host, the consecrated bread. We sing or pray aloud,
  **"Lamb of God, you take away the sins of the world,
    have mercy on us.
  Lamb of God, you take away the sins of the world,
    have mercy on us.
  Lamb of God, you take away the sins of the world,
    grant us peace."**

Communion
The priest raises the host and says aloud,
  "Behold the Lamb of God, behold him who takes away the sins of the world.
  Blessed are those called to the supper of the Lamb."

We join with him and say,
  "Lord, I am not worthy that you should enter under my roof, but only say the word and my soul shall be healed."

The priest receives Communion. Next, the deacon and the extraordinary ministers of Holy Communion and the members of the assembly receive Communion.

The priest, deacon, or extraordinary minister of Holy Communion holds up the host. We bow, and the priest, deacon, or extraordinary minister of Holy Communion says, "The Body of Christ." We respond, **"Amen."** We then receive the consecrated host in our hands or on our tongues.

If we are to receive the Blood of Christ, the priest, deacon, or extraordinary minister of Holy Communion holds up the cup containing the consecrated wine. We bow, and the priest, deacon, or extraordinary minister of Holy Communion says, "The Blood of Christ." We respond, **"Amen."** We take the cup in our hands and drink from it.

The Prayer after Communion
We stand as the priest invites us to pray, saying, "Let us pray." He prays the Prayer after Communion. We respond,
"Amen."

The Concluding Rites
We are sent forth to do good works,
praising and blessing the Lord.

Greeting

We stand. The priest greets us as we prepare to leave. He says, "The Lord be with you." We respond, **"And with your spirit."**

Final Blessing

The priest or deacon may invite us,
"Bow your heads and pray for God's blessing."
The priest blesses us, saying,
"May almighty God bless you: the Father, and the Son, and the Holy Spirit."
We respond, **"Amen."**

Dismissal of the People

The priest or deacon sends us forth, using these or similar words,
"Go in peace, glorifying the Lord by your life."
We respond,
"Thanks be to God."
We sing a hymn. The priest and the deacon kiss the altar. The priest, deacon, and other ministers bow to the altar and leave in procession.

The Sacrament of Reconciliation

Individual Rite

Greeting
Scripture Reading
Confession of Sins
    and Acceptance of Penance
Act of Contrition
Absolution
Closing Prayer

Communal Rite

Greeting
Scripture Reading
Homily
Examination of Conscience, a
    Litany of Contrition, and the
    Lord's Prayer
Individual Confession and Absolution
Closing Prayer

Key Teachings of the Catholic Church

The Mystery of God

Divine Revelation

Who am I?

You are a person created by God. God wants you to live in friendship with him on Earth and forever in Heaven.

How do we know this about ourselves?

God knows and loves all people. God wants us to know and love him too. God tells us about ourselves. God also tells us about himself.

How did God tell us?

God tells us in many ways. First, all the things God has created tell us about him. We see God's goodness and beauty in creation. Second, God came to us and he told us about himself. He told us the most when he sent his Son, Jesus Christ. God's Son became one of us and lived among us. He showed us who God is.

What is faith?

Faith is a gift from God. It helps us to know and to believe in God.

What is a mystery of faith?

A mystery of faith can never be known completely. We cannot know everything about God. We only know who God is because he told us about himself.

What is Divine Revelation?

God wants us to know about him. Divine Revelation is how he freely makes himself known to us. God has told us about himself and his plan for us. He has done this so that we can live in friendship with him and with one another forever.

What is Sacred Tradition?

The word *tradition* means "to pass on." The Church's Sacred Tradition passes on what God has told us. The Holy Spirit guides the Church to tell us about God.

Sacred Scripture

What is Sacred Scripture?

Sacred Scripture means "holy writings." Sacred Scripture are writings that tell God's story.

What is the Bible?

The Bible is God's Word. It is a holy book. The stories in the Bible teach about God. The Bible tells the stories about Jesus. When you listen to the Bible, you are listening to God.

What does it mean to say that the Bible is inspired?

This means that the Holy Spirit helped people write about God. The Holy Spirit helped the writers tell what God wants us to know about him.

What is the Old Testament?

The Old Testament is the first part of the Bible. It has forty-six books. They were written before the birth of Jesus. The Old Testament tells the story of creation. It tells about Adam and Eve. It tells about the promise, or Covenant, between God and his people.

What is the Covenant?

The Covenant is the promise that God and his people freely made. It is God's promise always to love and be kind to his people.

What are the writings of the prophets?

God chose people to speak in his name. These people are called the prophets. We read the message of the prophets in the Bible. The prophets remind God's people that God is faithful. They remind God's people to be faithful to the Covenant.

What is the New Testament?

The New Testament is the second part of the Bible. It has twenty-seven books. These books were inspired by the Holy Spirit. They were written during the time of the Apostles. They are about Jesus Christ. They tell about his saving work.

What are the Gospels?

The Gospels are the four books at the beginning of the New Testament. They tell the story of Jesus and his teachings. The four Gospels are Matthew, Mark, Luke, and John.

What are the letters of Saint Paul?

The letters of Saint Paul are in the New Testament. The letters teach about the Church. They tell how to follow Jesus. Some of these letters were written before the Gospels.

The Holy Trinity

Who is the Mystery of the Holy Trinity?

The Holy Trinity is the mystery of one God in three Persons—God the Father, God the Son, and God the Holy Spirit.

Who is God the Father?

God the Father is the First Person of the Holy Trinity.

Who is God the Son?

God the Son is Jesus Christ. He is the Second Person of the Holy Trinity. God the Father sent his Son to be one of us and live with us.

Who is God the Holy Spirit?

The Holy Spirit is the Third Person of the Holy Trinity. God sends us the Holy Spirit to help us to know and love God better. The Holy Spirit helps us live as children of God.

Divine Work of Creation

What does it mean to call God the Creator?

God is the Creator. He has made everyone and everything out of love. He has created everyone and everything without any help.

Who are angels?

Angels are spiritual beings. They do not have bodies like we do. Angels give glory to God at all times. They sometimes serve God by bringing his message to people.

Why are human beings special?

God creates every human being in his image and likeness. God shares his life with us. God wants us to be happy with him, forever.

What is the soul?

The soul is the spiritual part of a person. The soul will never die. It is the part of us that lives forever. It bears the image of God.

What is free will?

Free will is the power God gives us to choose between good and evil. Free will gives us the power to turn toward God.

What is Original Sin?

Original Sin is the sin of Adam and Eve. They chose to disobey God. As a result of Original Sin, death, sin, and suffering came into the world.

Jesus Christ, Son of God, Son of Mary

What is the Annunciation?

At the Annunciation the angel Gabriel came to Mary. The angel had a message for her. God had chosen her to be the Mother of his Son, Jesus.

What is the Incarnation?

The Incarnation is the Son of God becoming a man and still being God. Jesus Christ is true God and true man.

What does it mean that Jesus is Lord?

The word *lord* means "master or ruler." When we call Jesus "Lord," we mean that he is truly God.

What is the Paschal Mystery?

The Paschal Mystery is the Passion, Death, Resurrection, and Ascension of Jesus Christ. Jesus passed over from death into new and glorious life.

What is Salvation?

The word *salvation* means "to save." It is the saving of all people from sin and death through Jesus Christ.

What is the Resurrection?

The Resurrection is God's raising Jesus from the dead to new life.

What is the Ascension?

The Ascension is the return of the Risen Jesus to his Father in Heaven.

What is the Second Coming of Christ?

Christ will come again in glory at the end of time. This is the Second Coming of Christ. He will judge the living and the dead. This is the fulfillment of God's plan.

What does it mean that Jesus is the Messiah?

The word *messiah* means "anointed one." He is the Messiah. God promised to send the Messiah to save all people. Jesus is the Savior of the world.

The Mystery of the Church

What is the Church?

The word *church* means "those who are called together." The Church is the Body of Christ. It is the new People of God.

What does the Church do?

The Church tells all people the Good News of Jesus Christ. The Church invites all people to know, love, and serve Jesus.

What is the Body of Christ?

The Church is the Body of Christ on Earth. Jesus Christ is the Head of the Church and all baptized people are its members.

Who are the People of God?

The Church is the People of God. God invites all people to belong to the People of God. The People of God live as one family in God.

What is the Communion of Saints?

The Communion of Saints is all of the holy people that make up the Church. It is the faithful followers of Jesus on Earth. It is those who have died who are still becoming holier. It is also those who have died and are happy forever with God in Heaven.

What are the Marks of the Church?

There are four main ways to describe the Church. We call these the Four Marks of the Church. The Church is one, holy, catholic, and apostolic.

Who are the Apostles?

The Apostles were the disciples who Jesus chose. He sent them to preach the Gospel to the whole world in his name. Some of their names are Peter, Andrew, James, and John.

What is Pentecost?

Pentecost is the day the Holy Spirit came to the disciples of Jesus. This happened fifty days after the Resurrection. The work of the Church began on this day.

Who are the clergy?

The clergy are bishops, priests, and deacons. They have received the Sacrament of Holy Orders. They serve the whole Church.

What is the work of the pope?

Jesus Christ is the true Head of the Church. The pope and the bishops lead the Church in his name. The pope is the bishop of Rome. He is the successor to Saint Peter the Apostle, the first pope. The pope brings the Church together. The Holy Spirit guides the pope when he speaks about faith and about what Catholics believe.

What is the work of the bishops?

The other bishops are the successors of the other Apostles. They teach and lead the Church in their dioceses. The Holy Spirit always guides the pope and all of the bishops. He guides them when they make important decisions.

What is religious life?

Some men and women want to follow Jesus in a special way. They choose the religious life. They promise not to marry. They dedicate their whole lives to doing Jesus' work. They promise to live holy lives. They promise to live simply. They share what they have with others. They live together in groups and they promise to obey the rules of their community. They may lead quiet lives of prayer, or teach, or take care of people who are sick or poor.

Who are lay people?

Many people do not receive the Sacrament of Holy Orders. Many are not members of a religious community. These are lay people. Lay people follow Christ every day by what they do and say.

The Blessed Virgin Mary

Who is Mary?

God chose Mary to be the mother of his only Son, Jesus. Mary is the Mother of God. She is the Mother of Jesus. She is the Mother of the Church. Mary is the greatest saint.

What is the Immaculate Conception?

From the first moment of her being, Mary was preserved from sin. This special grace from God continued throughout her whole life. We call this the Immaculate Conception.

What is the Assumption of Mary?

At the end of her life on Earth, the Blessed Virgin Mary was taken body and soul into Heaven. Mary hears our prayers. She tells her Son what we need. She reminds us of the life that we all hope to share when Christ, her Son, comes again in glory.

Life Everlasting

What is eternal life?
Eternal life is life after death. At death the soul leaves the body. It passes into eternal life.

What is Heaven?
Heaven is living with God and with Mary and all the saints in happiness forever after we die.

What is the Kingdom of God?
The Kingdom of God is also called the Kingdom of Heaven. It is all people and creation living in friendship with God.

What is Purgatory?
Purgatory is the chance to grow in love for God after we die so we can live forever in heaven.

What is Hell?
Hell is life away from God and the saints forever after death.

Celebration of the Christian Life and Mystery

Liturgy and Worship

What is worship?
Worship is the praise we give God. The Church worships God in the liturgy.

What is liturgy?
The liturgy is the Church's worship of God. It is the work of the Body of Christ. Christ is present by the power of the Holy Spirit.

What is the liturgical year?
The liturgical year is the name of the seasons and feasts that make up the Church's year of worship. The main seasons of the Church year are Advent, Christmas, Lent, and Easter. The Triduum is the three holy days just before Easter. The rest of the liturgical year is called Ordinary Time.

The Sacraments

What are the sacraments?
The sacraments are the seven signs of God's love for us that Jesus gave the Church. We share in God's love when we celebrate the sacraments.

What are the Sacraments of Christian Initiation?
The Sacraments of Christian Initiation are Baptism, Confirmation, and Eucharist.

What is the Sacrament of Baptism?
Baptism joins us to Christ. It makes us members of the Church. We receive the gift of the Holy Spirit. Original Sin and our personal sins are forgiven. Through Baptism, we belong to Christ.

What is the Sacrament of Confirmation?
At Confirmation we receive the gift of the Holy Spirit. The Holy Spirit strengthens us to live our Baptism.

What is the Sacrament of Eucharist?
In the Eucharist, we join with Christ. We give thanksgiving, honor, and glory to God the Father. Through the power of the Holy Spirit, the bread and wine become the Body and Blood of Jesus Christ.

Why do we have to participate at Sunday Mass?

Catholics participate in the Eucharist on Sundays and holy days of obligation. Sunday is the Lord's Day. Participating at the Mass, and receiving Holy Communion, the Body and Blood of Christ, when we are old enough, are necessary for Christians.

What is the Mass?

The Mass is the main celebration of the Church. At Mass we worship God. We listen to God's Word. We celebrate and share in the Eucharist.

What are the Sacraments of Healing?

The two Sacraments of Healing are the Sacrament of Penance and Reconciliation and the Sacrament of Anointing of the Sick.

What is confession?

Confession is telling our sins to a priest in the Sacrament of Penance. Confession is another name for the Sacrament of Penance.

What is contrition?

Contrition is being truly sorry for our sins. We want to make up for the hurt our sins have caused. We do not want to sin again.

What is penance?

A penance is a prayer or act of kindness. The penance we do shows that we are truly sorry for our sins. The priest gives us a penance to help repair the hurt caused by our sin.

What is absolution?

Absolution is the forgiveness of sins by God through the words and actions of the priest.

What is the Sacrament of Anointing of the Sick?

The Sacrament of Anointing of the Sick is one of the two Sacraments of Healing. We receive this sacrament when we are very sick, old, or dying. This sacrament helps make our faith and trust in God strong.

What are the Sacraments at the Service of Communion?

Holy Orders and Matrimony, or Marriage, are the two Sacraments at the Service of Communion. People who receive these sacraments serve God.

What is the Sacrament of Holy Orders?

In this sacrament, baptized men are consecrated as bishops, priests, or deacons. They serve the whole Church. They serve in the name and person of Christ.

Who is a bishop?

A bishop is a priest. He receives the fullness of the Sacrament of Holy Orders. He is a successor to the Apostles. He leads and serves in a diocese. He teaches and leads worship in the name of Jesus.

Who is a priest?

A priest is a baptized man who receives the Sacrament of Holy Orders. Priests work with their bishops. The priest teaches about the Catholic faith. He celebrates Mass. Priests help to guide the Church.

Who is a deacon?

A deacon is ordained to help bishops and priests. He is not a priest. He is ordained to serve the Church.

What is the Sacrament of Matrimony?

In the Sacrament of Matrimony, or Marriage, a baptized man and a baptized woman make a lifelong promise. They promise to serve the Church as a married couple. They promise to love each other. They show Christ's love to others.

What are the sacramentals of the Church?

Sacramentals are objects and blessings the Church uses. They help us worship God.

Life in the Spirit

The Moral Life

Why did God create us?

God created us to give honor and glory to him. God created us to live a life of blessing with him here on Earth and forever in Heaven.

What does it mean to live a moral life?

God wants us to be happy. He gives us the gift of his grace. When we accept God's gift by living the way Jesus taught us, we are being moral.

What is the Great Commandment?

Jesus taught us to love God above all else. He taught us to love our neighbor as ourselves. This is the path to happiness.

What are the Ten Commandments?

The Ten Commandments are the laws that God gave Moses. They teach us to live as God's people. They teach us to love God, others, and ourselves. The Commandments are written on the hearts of all people.

What are the Beatitudes?

The Beatitudes are teachings of Jesus. They tell us what real happiness is. The Beatitudes tell us about the Kingdom of God. They help us live as followers of Jesus. They help us keep God at the center of our lives.

What are the Works of Mercy?

God's love and kindness is at work in the world. This is what mercy is. Human works of mercy are acts of loving kindness. We reach out to people. We help them with what they need for their bodies and their spirits.

What are the Precepts of the Church?

The Precepts of the Church are five rules. These rules help us worship God and grow in love of God and our neighbor.

Holiness of Life and Grace

What is holiness?

Holiness is life with God. Holy people are in the right relationship with God, with people, and with all of creation.

What is grace?

Grace is the gift of God sharing of his life and love with us.

What is sanctifying grace?

Sanctifying grace is the grace we receive at Baptism. It is a free gift of God, given by the Holy Spirit.

What are the Gifts of the Holy Spirit?

The seven Gifts of the Holy Spirit help us to live our Baptism. They are wisdom, understanding, right judgment, courage, knowledge, reverence, and wonder and awe.

The Virtues

What are the virtues?

The virtues are spiritual powers or habits. The virtues help us to do what is good.

What are the most important virtues?

The most important virtues are the three virtues of faith, hope, and love. These virtues are gifts from God. They help us keep God at the center of our lives.

What is conscience?

Every person has a conscience. It is a gift God gives to every person. It helps us know and judge what is right and what is wrong. Our consciences move us to do good and avoid evil.

Evil and Sin

What is evil?

Evil is the harm we choose to do to one another and to God's creation.

What is temptation?

Temptations are feelings, people, and things that try to get us to turn away from God's love and not live a holy life.

What is sin?

Sin is freely choosing to do or say something that we know God does not want us to do or say.

What is mortal sin?

A mortal sin is doing or saying something on purpose that is very bad. A mortal sin is against what God wants us to do or say. When we commit a mortal sin, we lose sanctifying grace.

What are venial sins?

Venial sins are sins that are less serious than mortal sins. They weaken our love for God and for one another. They make us less holy.

Christian Prayer

What is prayer?

Prayer is talking to and listening to God. When we pray, we raise our minds and hearts to God the Father, Son, and Holy Spirit.

What is the Our Father?

The Lord's Prayer, or Our Father, is the prayer of all Christians. Jesus taught his disciples the Our Father. Jesus gave this prayer to the Church. When we pray the Our Father, we come closer to God and to his Son, Jesus Christ. The Our Father helps us become like Jesus.

What kinds of prayer are there?

Some kinds of prayer use words that we say aloud or quietly in our hearts. Some silent prayers use our imagination to bring us closer to God. Another silent prayer is simply being with God.

Glossary

angels
[page 49]

_____

- - - - - - - - - - - - - - - - - - - -

_____ are God's messengers and helpers.

Baptism
[page 93]

_____

- - - - - - - - - - - - - - - - - - - -

_____ is the first sacrament that we celebrate. In Baptism, we receive the gift of God's life and become members of the Church.

believe
[page 21]

_____

- - - - - - - - - - - - - - - - - - - -

To _____ means to have faith in God.

Bible
[page 13]

_____

- - - - - - - - - - - - - - - - - - - -

The _____ is the written Word of God.

Catholics
[page 73]

_____

- - - - - - - - - - - - - - - - - - - -

_____ are followers of Jesus and members of the Catholic Church.

charity
[page 208]

_____

- - - - - - - - - - - - - - - - - - - -

_____ is loving others as God loves us.

children of God
[page 201]

_____

- - - - - - - - - - - - - - - - - - - -

All people are _____, created in God's image.

Christians
[page 157]

_____

- - - - - - - - - - - - - - - - - - - -

_____ believe in Jesus Christ and live as he taught.

Church
[page 73]

_____

- -

The _____ is the People of God who believe in Jesus and live as his followers.

Church's year
[page 85]

_____

- -

The _____
is made up of four main seasons. They are Advent, Christmas, Lent, and Easter.

community
[page 181]

_____

- -

A _____ is a group of people who respect and care for one another.

counsel
[page 64]

_____

- -

_____ is another word for the help that a good teacher gives us. Counsel is a gift of the Holy Spirit.

courage
[page 48]

_____

- -

The virtue of _____
helps us to trust in God and live our faith.

Creator
[page 29]

_____

- -

God is the _____.
He created out of love and without any help.

cross
[page 57]

_____

- -

Jesus died on a _____ so that we could live forever in Heaven.

disciples
[page 57]

_____

- -

_____ are followers of Jesus.

Easter
[page 85]

_____

- -

_____ is the season when
we celebrate that Jesus is risen.

Eucharist
[page 137]

_____

- -

The _____
is the sacrament in which we receive the Body and
Blood of Christ.

faith
[page 21]

_____

- -

_____ is a gift from God. It
helps us to know God and to believe in him.

faithful
[page 12]

_____

- - - - - - - - - - - - - - - - - - - -

Good friends of Jesus are _____
to him. They are loyal to him.

fidelity
[page 108]

_____

- -

Parents demonstrate _____
when they love and care for their children.

Galilee
[page 145]

_____

- -

_____ was one of the
main places where Jesus taught and helped people.

generosity
[page 20]

We share our things with others. We show
_____

- -

_____ to them.

gentleness
[page 200]

Gentle people act calmly. They treat all people
_____

- -

with _____.

glory
[page 201]

_____ is another word for praise.

goodness
[page 100]

_____ is a sign that we are living our Baptism. When we are good to people, we honor God.

Gospel
[page 101]

The _____ is the Good News that Jesus told us about God's love.

Great Commandment
[page 181]

The _____ is to love God above all else and to love others as we love ourselves.

Holy Family
[page 37]

The _____ is the family of Jesus, Mary, and Joseph.

Holy Spirit
[page 65]

The _____ is the Third Person of the Holy Trinity.

Holy Trinity
[page 65]

The _____ is one God in Three Divine Persons—God the Father, God the Son, and God the Holy Spirit.

honor
[page 173]

We _____ people when we treat them with great respect.

hope
[page 56]

The virtue of _____ helps us to remember that one day we may live in happiness with God forever in Heaven.

hospitality
[page 92]

We demonstrate _____ when we welcome others as God's children.

humility
[page 216]

_____ helps us know that all good things come from God.

image of God
[page 29]

We are created in the _____ .

joy
[page 192]

We live with _____ when we recognize that true happiness comes from knowing and following Jesus.

justice
[page 180]

We practice _____ when we treat people fairly.

kindness
[page 36]

We live the virtue of _____ by treating others as we want to be treated.

Kingdom of God
[page 193]

The _____ is Heaven. Heaven is happiness with God forever.

knowledge
[page 164]

The gift of _____ helps you to know and to follow God's rules.

marriage
[page 109]

A _____ is the lifelong promise of love made by a man and a woman to live as a family.

Mass
[page 137]

The _____ is the most important celebration of the Church.

Matrimony
[page 109]

_____ is the sacrament that Catholics celebrate when they marry.

miracle
[page 145]

A _____ is something only God can do. It is a sign of God's love.

Our Father
[page 217]

The _____ is the prayer Jesus taught his disciples.

parable
[page 209]

Jesus often told a _____ to help people to know and love God better.

patience
[page 120]

We act with _____ when we listen carefully to others.

peace
[page 128]

_____

- -

We live as _____ makers
when we forgive those who have hurt us.

perseverance
[page 136]

_____

- -

_____ helps us to
live our faith when it is difficult.

prayer
[page 121]

_____

- -

_____ is listening and
talking to God.

prudence
[page 84]

_____

- -

_____ helps us ask advice
from others when making important decisions.

respect
[page 173]

_____

- -

We show people _____ when
we love them because they are children of God.

Resurrection
[page 57]

God's raising Jesus from the dead to new life is
_____

- -

called the _____.

reverence
[page 72]

_____

- -

We show _____
to others when we honor them and give them great
respect.

Sacraments
[page 93]

_____

- -

The _____ are
the seven signs and celebrations of God's love that
Jesus gave the Church.

sin
[page 129]

_____ is choosing to do or say something that we know is against God's laws.

Son of God
[page 37]

Jesus is the _____.

temperance
[page 172]

_____ helps us to know the difference between what we need and what we just want to have.

Ten Commandments
[page 165]

The _____ are the ten laws that God has given us to help us live as children of God.

understanding
[page 156]

God the Holy Spirit gives us the gift of _____. Stories in the Bible help us understand God's love for us.

wisdom
[page 144]

_____ helps us to know what God wants us to do. It helps us to live a holy life.

wonder
[page 28]

_____ is a gift from God to help us know how good He is.

worship
[page 165]

We _____ God when we love and honor God more than anyone and anything else.

Index

Credits

Cover Illustration: Marcia Adams Ho

PHOTO CREDITS

Frontmatter: Page 6, © Laurence Monneret/Getty Images; 7, © Ladushka/Shutterstock.

Chapter 1: Page 11, © Andersen Ross, 17, © Ken Seet/Corbis; 18, © Ocean/Corbis.

Chapter 2: Page 19, © Fever Images/Jupiterimages; 26, © Asia Images Group Pte Ltd/Alamy.

Chapter 3: Page 30, © Dmitriy Shironosov/Shutterstock.com; 34, © Jupiterimages.

Chapter 4: Page 39, © Bounce/Getty Images; 39, © Design Pics Inc./Alamy; 39, © Fuse/Getty Images; 42, © Design Pics Inc./Alamy.

Chapter 5: Page 47, © Roger Cracknell 01/classic / Alamy; 50, © LWA/Jay Newman/Jupiterimages; 51, © Jupiterimages; 53, © Plush Studios/Jupiterimages; 54, © Design Pics/Kristy-Anne Glubish/Getty Images.

Chapter 6: Page 56, © AFP/Getty Images; 57, © Bill Wittman; 61, © Jose Luis Pelaez Inc/Jupiterimages; 62, © kali9/iStockphoto.

Chapter 7: Page 63, iofoto/Shutterstock; 64, © The Crosiers/Gene Plaisted, OSC; 66, © Tischenko Irina /Shutterstock; 67, © Fuse/Jupiterimages; 67, © Bruce Forster/Getty Images; 67, © Fuse/Jupiterimages; 69, © Bill Wittman; 70, © Blend Images/Alamy.

Chapter 8: Page 77, © Design Pics/Don Hammond/Jupiterimages; 78, © Blend Images/Alamy.

Chapter 9: Page 83, © Dorling Kindersley/Jupiterimages; 89, © Tetra Images/Jupiterimages; 90, © AFP/Getty Images.

Chapter 10: Page 93, © Dmitry Naumov / Shutterstock; 94, © Bill Wittman; 95, © Ted Foxx/Alamy; 98, © a la france/Alamy.

Chapter 11: Page 102, © Tim Graham/Getty Images; 106, © Michael Hitoshi/Jupiterimages.

Chapter 12: Page 107, © OJO Images/Jupiterimages; 108, © Jose Luis Pelaez Inc/Jupiterimages; 108, © Fancy/Veer/Corbis/Jupiterimages; 109, © Jupiterimages; 109, © Monkey Business Images/Shutterstock; 113, © Fuse/Jupiterimages; 114, © Purestock/Getty Images.

Chapter 13: Page 121, © Brand X Pictures/Jupiterimages; 125, © The Crosiers/Gene Plaisted, OSC; 126, © Fuse/Jupiterimages.

Chapter 14: Page 128, © AFP/Getty Images; 131, © Steve Gorton/Getty Images; 133, © Myrleen Ferguson Cate/Photo Edit; 134, © moodboard/Alamy.

Chapter 15: Page 135, © SW Productions/Jupiterimages; 136, © Design Pics Inc./Alamy; 141, © Stockbyte/Jupiterimages; 142, © Bill Wittman.

Chapter 16: Page 143, © Juice Images/Jupiterimages; 144, © CRS; 144, © Jim Stipe/CRS; 144, © Jim Stipe/CRS; 147, © Ariel Skelley/Jupiterimages; 147, © SW Productions/Jupiterimages; 147, © Andersen Ross/Jupiterimages; 149, © Design Pics Inc./Alamy; 150, © Juice Images/Alamy.

Chapter 17: Page 155, © Danita Delimont/Alamy; 161, © Inspirestock Inc./Alamy; 162, © Tony Freeman/Photo Edit.

Chapter 18: Page 164, © 501room/Shutterstock; 164, © Ritu Manoj Jethani/Shutterstock; 164, © Neil Jacobs/Getty Images; 165, © sonya etchison/Shutterstock; 166, © Colorblind/Jupiterimages; 166, © George Doyle/Jupiterimages; 166, © Daniel Pangbourne/Jupiterimages; 169, © Stockbyte/Jupiterimages; 170, © Jupiterimages.

Chapter 19: Page 171, ©Monkey Business Images/Shutterstock; 172, © Tony Freeman/Photo Edit; 173, © Karl Kost/Alamy; 173, © SW Productions/Getty Images; 177, © Paul Burns/Jupiterimages; 178, © BananaStock/Jupiterimages.

Chapter 20: Page 179, © Zigy Kaluzny/Getty Images; 181, © Fuse/Jupiterimages; 181, © Tom Merton/Jupiterimages; 181, © Colin Hawkins/Jupiterimages; 185, © Brand X Pictures/Jupiterimages; 186, © Ocean/Corbis.

Chapter 21: Page 191, © Stockbyte/Getty Images; 192, © Photograph courtesy of the Pontifical Mission Societies; 192, © taelove7/Shutterstock; 195, © Dmitriy Shironosov/Shutterstock; 195, © GlowImage/Alamy; 195, © Blend Images/Alamy; 197, © Digital Vision/Jupiterimages; 198, © Michael Newman / Photo Edit.

Chapter 22: Page 200, © William Thomas Cain/Getty Images; 202, © Thomas M Perkins/Shutterstock; 202, © laszlo a. lim/Shutterstock; 205, © Zdorov Kirill Vladimirovich/Shutterstock; 206, © Dave & Les Jacobs/Jupiterimages.

Chapter 23: Page 213, © Bill Wittman 214, © Design Pics/SW Productions/Jupiterimages.

Chapter 24: Page 215, © Image Source/Jupiterimages; 216, © Jean-Claude FRANCOLON/Gamma-Rapho via Getty Images; 216, © Luciano Mortula /Shutterstock; 219, © Peter Zander/Getty Images; 221, © ONOKY - Photononstop/Alamy; 222, © Jupiterimages.

Liturgical Seasons: Page 225, © Design Pics Inc./Alamy; 226, © Chris Salvo/Getty Images; 226, © sodapix sodapix/Getty Images; 226, © ATTILA KISBENEDEK/AFP/Getty Images; 226, © The Crosiers/Gene Plaisted, OSC; 226, © ClassicStock/Alamy; 227, © Stockbyte/Jupiterimages; 227, © The Crosiers/Gene Plaisted, OSC; 227, © The Crosiers/Gene Plaisted, OSC; 227, © The Crosiers/Gene Plaisted, OSC; 229, © McPHOTO / SHU; 231, © The Crosiers/Gene Plaisted, OSC; 233, © The Crosiers/Gene Plaisted, OSC; 235, © Serp/Shutterstock; 235, © Cathy Baxter/Private Collection/The Bridgeman Art Library; 236, © Spencer Grant / Photo Edit; 237, © The Crosiers/Gene Plaisted, OSC; 239, © The Crosiers/Gene Plaisted, OSC; 241, © AP Photo/The Miami Herald, Walter Michot; 241, © Amanda Brown/Star Ledger/Corbis; 243, © Dejan Ristovski /Getty Images; 245, © asharkyu/Shutterstock; 245, © Bill Wittman; 245, © The Crosiers/Gene Plaisted, OSC; 247, © Bill Wittman; 249, © The Crosiers/Gene Plaisted, OSC; 249, © Bill Wittman; 251, © Ocean/Corbis; 251, © Bill Wittman; 251, © Cornelia Doerr/Getty Images; 253, © The Crosiers/Gene Plaisted, OSC; 255, © The Crosiers/Gene Plaisted, OSC; 255, © Stephanie Neal Photography/Getty Images.

Backmatter: Page 257, © Fuse/Jupiterimages; 259, © Blend Images/Alamy; 262, © Bill Wittman; 263, © Bill Wittman; 264, © Bill Wittman; 265, © Bill Wittman; 266, © Bill Wittman; 267, © Bill Wittman; 269, © Bill Wittman.

ILLUSTRATION CREDITS

Listed from Top to Bottom; Left to Right

Frontmatter: Page 8,

Chapter 1: Page 12, Q2A Media; **14-15 Julia Woolf**

Chapter 2: Page 20, Q2A Media; 21, Julia Woolf; 22, Q2A Media; 23, Q2A Media; 25, Q2A Media.

Chapter 3: Page 27, Q2A Media; 28, Kristin Sorra; 29, Q2A Media; 32, Q2A Media; 33, Q2A Media.

Chapter 4: Page 35, Julia Woolf, 36, Q2A Media; 37, Julia Woolf; 38, Julia Woolf; 41, Q2A Media.

Chapter 5: Page 48, Q2A Media; 49, Julia Woolf.

Chapter 6: Page 55, Julia Woolf; 58-**59**, Julia Woolf.

Chapter 7: Page 64, Q2A Media; 66, Q2A Media.

Chapter 8: Page 71, Q2A Media; 72, Q2A Media; 73, Julia Woolf; 75, Q2A Media.

Chapter 9: Page 84, Q2A Media; 85, Q2A Media; 86, Q2A Media; 87, Q2A Media; 88, Q2A Media.

Chapter 10: Page 91, Julia Woolf; 92, Q2A Media; 94, Q2A Media.

Chapter 11: Page 99, Julia Woolf; 100, Q2A Media; 101, Julia Woolf; 103, Q2A Media; 104, Q2A Media; 105, Q2A Media.

Chapter 12: Page 110, Q2A Media; 111, Julia Woolf.

Chapter 13: Page 120, Q2A Media; 122, Q2A Media; 123, Q2A Media.

Chapter 14: Page 127, Sole Otero; 129, Q2A Media; 130, Q2A Media; 132, Q2A Media.

Chapter 15: Page 137, Q2A Media; 139, Julia Woolf.

Chapter 16: Page 145, Lyn Boyer; 146, Julia Woolf.

Chapter 17: Page 156, Q2A Media; 158-**9**, Julia Woolf.

Chapter 18: Page 163, Ivanke and Lola; 167, Q2A Media.

Chapter 19: Page 174, Q2A Media; 175, Rémy Simard.

Chapter 20: Page 180, Colleen Madden; 182, Q2A Media; 183, Q2A Media.

Chapter 21: Page 193, Kristin Sorra; 194, Julia Woolf.

Chapter 22: Page 199, Julia Woolf; 201, Q2A Media.

Chapter 23: Page 207, Julia Woolf; 208, Q2A Media; 209, Q2A Media; 210, Julia Woolf; 211, Rémy Simard.

Chapter 24: Page 217, Q2A Media.

Liturgical Seasons: Page 234, Pamela Becker; 244, Ivanke and Lola; 256, Ivanke and Lola.